DOS

Made Simple

Made Simple *Computer Books*

- **easy to follow**
- **jargon free**
- **practical**
- **task based**
- **easy steps**

All you want are the **basics**. You don't want to be bothered with all the advanced stuff, or be engulfed in technical mumbo jumbo . You have neither the time nor the interest in knowing about every feature, function or command and you don't want to wade through big computer books on the subject or stumble through the maze of information in the manuals

The **MADE SIMPLE** series is **for you!**

You want to **learn quickly what's essential** and **how** to do things with a particular piece of software. You are:

- **a Secretary** or **temp** who wants to **get the job done**, **quickly** and **efficiently**

- **a Manager**, without the time to learn all about the software but who wants to **produce** **letters, memos, reports** or **spreadsheets**

- someone **working from home** using the software, who needs a **self-teaching** approach, that gives **results fast**, with the least confusion.

By a combination of **tutorial approach**, with **tasks to do**, and **easy steps** the **MADE SIMPLE** series of Computer Books stands above all others.

See the complete series at your **local bookstore now,** or in case of difficulty, contact:

Reed Book Services Ltd., Orders Dept, PO Box 5, Rushden, Northants, NN10 9YX. Tel 0933 58521. Fax 0933 50284. Credit card sales 0933 410511.

Series titles:

AmiPro	Moira Stephen	0 7506 2067 6
Excel	Stephen Morris	0 7506 2070 6
Lotus 1-2-3	Ian Robertson	0 7506 2066 8
MS-Dos	Ian Sinclair	0 7506 2069 2
MS-Works	P. K. McBride	0 7506 2065 X
Windows	P. K. McBride	0 7506 2072 2
Word	Keith Brindley	0 7506 2071 4
WordPerfect	Stephen Copestake	0 7506 2068 4

DOS
Made Simple

Ian Sinclair

MADE SIMPLE
BOOKS

Made Simple
An imprint of Butterworth-Heinemann Ltd
Linacre House, Jordan Hill, Oxford OX2 8DP

℞ A member of the Reed Elsevier group

OXFORD	LONDON	BOSTON	
MUNICH	NEW DELHI	SINGAPORE	SYDNEY
TOKYO	TORONTO	WELLINGTON	

First published 1994
© Ian Sinclair 1994

TRADEMARKS/REGISTERED TRADEMARKS
Computer hardware and software brand names mentioned in this book are
protected by their respective trademarks and are acknowledged.

British Library Cataloguing in Publication Data
A catalogue record for this book is available from the British Library

ISBN 0 7506 2069 2

Typeset by P.K.McBride, Southampton
Archetype, Bash Casual, Cotswold and Gravity fonts from Advanced
Graphics Ltd

Icons designed by Sarah Ward © 1994

Printed and bound in Great Britain
by Scotprint, Musselburgh, Scotland

Contents

Preface

The computer is about as simple as a spacecraft, and who ever let an untrained spaceman loose? You pick up a manual that weighs more than your birth-weight, open it and find that its written in computerspeak. You see messages on the screen that look like code and the thing even makes noises. No wonder that you feel it's your lucky day if everything goes right. What do you do if everything goes wrong? Give up.

Training helps. Being able to type helps. Experience helps. This book helps, by providing training and assisting with experience. It can't help you if you always manage to hit the wrong keys, but it can tell you which are the right ones and what to do when you hit the wrong ones. After some time, even the dreaded manual will start to make sense, just because you know what the writers are wittering on about.

Computing is not black magic. You don't need luck or charms, just a bit of understanding. The problem is that the programs that are used nowadays look simple but aren't. Most of them are crammed with features you don't need – but how do you know what you don't need? This book shows you what is essential and guides you through it. You will know how to make an action work and why. The less essential bits can wait – and once you start to use a program with confidence you can tackle these bits for yourself.

The writers of this series have all been through it. We know your time is valuable, and you don't want to waste it. You don't buy books on computer subjects to read jokes or be told that you are a dummy. You want to find what you need and be shown how to achieve it. Here, at last, you can.

1 Why use DOS?

Controlling the machine

A computer is helpless without a program, as helpless as a gramophone without records. Unlike a gramophone, the computer needs a sort of master program to run all the others. That's the program called DOS, and for the PC machine you will use either MS-DOS or a DOS that is almost identical.

Until DOS is loaded and running you cannot control the computer in any way. Only a very few keys have any effect, and these should not be used unless you know what you are doing.

You know that DOS is ready for a command when its prompt message appears – this consists of a drive letter and a chevron sign.

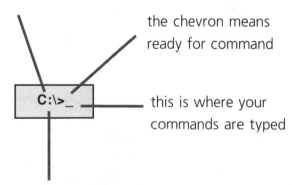

the letter for the
disk drive

the chevron means
ready for command

`C:\>_`

this is where your
commands are typed

the colon sign means that the letter
it follows is a drive letter

Basic steps

1 The computer is switched on.

2 It finds the MS-DOS program files on the hard drive or on a floppy disk

3 It loads in DOS and starts running it

4 You know when DOS is ready when you see the prompt message.

5 DOS allows you to issue commands to the computer

This action of loading in the MS-DOS (or PC-DOS or DR-DOS) files is called **booting**. It's a word you need to learn, because booting is when the machine is made ready for you.

Problems

- When the machine is ready to read in MS-DOS the loudspeaker will beep once to remind you that all is well.

- Sometimes you need to re-boot when an error causes the machine to lock up (not responding to the keyboard). You don't need to switch off to do this, because it can normally be done by pressing the **[Ctrl]- [Alt]-[Del]** keys to-gether.

- Sometimes when the machine does not respond this is because it is working hard. Do not be too quick to reboot – learn when there are actions that take time.

The loudspeaker beeps twice. This usually means that something important has changed, a new disk drive has been installed, perhaps.

Needs expert help.

You get the System Disk message.

> **Non-system disk or disk error**

Either your hard drive has failed or you have left a floppy disk in the A: drive.

The screen is full of printing.

Type the letters CLS and press the [Enter] key.

The prompt message is not C:\>, but the letter C appears.

> **C:\Friday 4 Mar 94>**

Not a problem – the appearance of the prompt can be changed, and someone has changed it.

Tip
___

If the screen is full of words, just type CLS and press the [Enter] key.

Using disk drives

The hard drive is inside the computer and it contains all the important programs that you use. It also contains data like your word-processed letters. Each program and each set of data is a file, and files are identified by their names.

Floppy disks nowadays are the 3.5" type. They are used to distribute programs that you buy and to hold copies of your data. These data copies are called backup. You need to know how to switch between the hard disk and a floppy disk.

Modern computers will be logged on to the hard disk automatically when you boot them. Very few machines use only a floppy drive nowadays.

1 Put a floppy disk into the A: drive. On modern computers this is the only floppy drive.

2 With the computer showing its prompt sign, type

   A:

   and press **[Enter]**.

3 This makes MS-DOS use the A: drive – you are logged-on to A:.

4 Now type

   C:

   and press **[Enter]** again. You are now logged back to the hard disk drive.

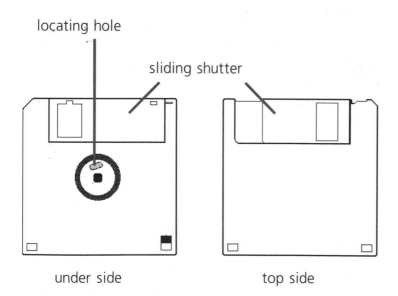

locating hole

sliding shutter

under side   top side

4

- If you try to log on to a floppy in the A: drive when there is no disk in the drive you will get an error message.

- A floppy disk will go completely into its drive only if it is the right way round. That means top side up, and metal shutter first into the drive. There is a slight resistance, so you have to push gently to make the disk click into place. If there is too much resistance, you're holding it the wrong way round.

- Don't take a floppy disk out of its drive while the drive-light is shining. Wait until the light goes out.

- Don't use damaged disks – if the metal shutter becomes bent, throw the disk away.

Hard disks are reliable but, like your car, they will fail some day. When that day comes you will be glad that you kept backup copies on floppy disks. If you have copies of all your programs and all your data on floppy disks you are much less likely to suffer loss of information when (not if) the hard disk fails.

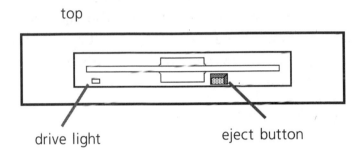

top

drive light   eject button

Never try to eject a disk except by pressing the eject button. If the button jams, get expert help. If you try to pull a disk out using pliers you will damage the drive as well as the disk.

Floppy drives are comparatively cheap, but they have a long life and they are almost fault-free. That's more than can ever be said for computer users.

Remember that you will use floppy disks for long-term storage – they should be stored in a cool dry place, well away from the two main enemies of sunlight and magnets.

Entering commands

All commands, including logging-on to another drive, are carried out when you press the **[Enter]** key. There are two – one marked **Enter**, the other marked with a hooked arrow. You can use whichever one is convenient.

You will probably find that your keyboard has a key marked **[Alt]** on the left side of the spacebar, and another key marked **[Alt Gr]** on the right side. For many actions, these are identical, but some programs pay no attention to the **[Alt Gr]** key. It's best not to get into the habit of using it.

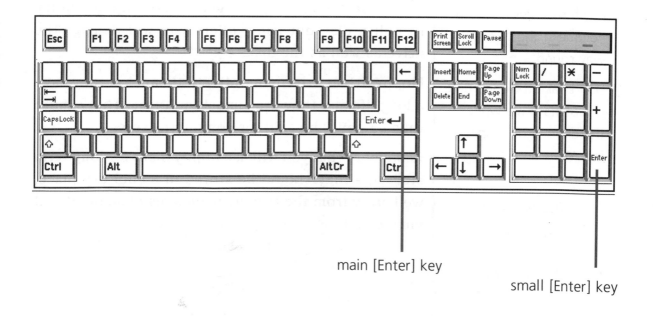

main [Enter] key

small [Enter] key

Basic steps

☐ **To run a program from a floppy disk:**

1 Make sure the correct disk is in the drive. Log on to the drive (type

    A:

and press [Enter]).

2 Type the program name and press [Enter] again.

3 The program will start running.

You must type the program name 100% correctly. There is no nearly-right – you have to be exactly right.

Take note

A really important point about using a hard disk is knowing how to move from one directory to another – we'll look at that in detail later in Section 3.

Running programs

To run a program, you need to know the filename that it uses. You also need to know where it is located on the hard disk. Both pieces of information need to be 100% correct otherwise the program simply won't run. Near enough is not good enough.

The big difference, as far as the hard disk is concerned, is that the disk is divided into sections called directories. You can think of a directory as a unit like a floppy disk. If the program that you want to run is not in the directory you are using you can't run it – for exceptions to this see later.

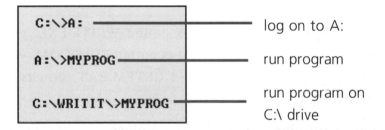

```
C:\>A:                     log on to A:

A:\>MYPROG                 run program

C:\WRITIT\>MYPROG          run program on
                           C:\ drive
```

You can run programs on the hard disk without needing to change to the directory that holds the program, but you must include the name of the directory as part of the filename. We'll look at this later, but the important point for the moment is that you must get to know your hard disk well – you need to know the name of each directory. The simplest way of ensuring this is to print out all the names and we'll look later at how this can be done.

Program names

Once a program is running, it takes over. All the commands that you use must be the commands of that program, and these will not be the same as the commands of MS-DOS, though some will be similar.

When a program ends, usually when you select a Quit or Exit option, you will see the MS-DOS prompt again. It should be just as it was before you started the program running.

A directory listing, see later, shows which files are program or batch files. All of these COM, EXE or BAT files will make programs run. You do not need to type this part of the name.

For example, if a program is called WRITE.EXE, you type only WRITE to run it. If it is called EDIT.COM, you type only EDIT. If it is called GETEM.BAT, you type only GETEM.

Some programs cannot be run unless you are using Windows – you will get a message if you try to run one using only DOS .

Points

❑ All programs are identified by name, and program names are all easy to identify. The name is in two parts, separated by a dot, and the name you need to type is the part before the dot.

❑ The three letters following the dot show that the file is a program. They can be EXE, COM or BAT.

❑ EXE is used for larger programs, which are the most common nowadays. COM is used for short programs. BAT is for files that contains MS-DOS commands for running programs.

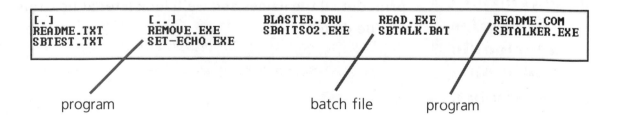

```
[.]              [..]            BLASTER.DRU     READ.EXE       README.COM
README.TXT       REMOUE.EXE      SBAITS02.EXE    SBTALK.BAT     SBTALKER.EXE
SBTEST.TXT       SET-ECHO.EXE
```

        program   batch file   program

Menus in programs

□ Nearly all modern programs that use DOS work with menus of the type illustrated here. In this example, the File menu is being used, and the Exit item is being selected to end the program.

Some older programs expect you to use keys for menu actions, such as **[Alt]-[F]** for **File** menu and **[Alt]-[X]** for **Exit**. **[Alt]-[X]** means pressing the **[Alt]** and the **[X]** key together.

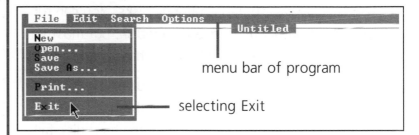

menu bar of program

selecting Exit

Most modern programs allow you to use a mouse, pointing the arrow at the item and clicking the mouse button.

There is a program called DOSSHELL which was supplied with MS-DOS 5.0 and 6.0, which allows you to control DOS actions using a mouse. We'll mention DOSSHELL throughout this book because it makes it easier to use DOS – but it is now supplied only to order.

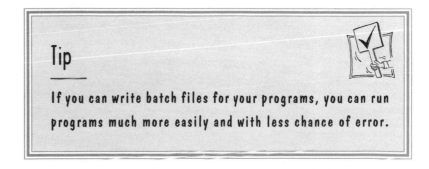

Tip

If you can write batch files for your programs, you can run programs much more easily and with less chance of error.

Summary

❑ A computer needs programs, its software, to carry out any task. A master program called DOS (usually MS-DOS) must be present before any other programs can be run.

❑ Programs are distributed on floppy disks. You can run some short programs from a floppy disk, but most will need to be stored and run from the hard disk.

❑ Floppy disks are also used to keep copies of your data (letters, accounts, drawings etc.) – these are backup copies. They will be essential when the hard disk fails.

❑ All commands, including running programs, require you to type the command and press the [Enter] key.

❑ If you want to run a program from a floppy disk, you need to have the correct disk in the drive. If you want to run a program from a hard disk, you must locate the correct hard disk directory.

❑ Get to know the names of your directories, and what programs they contain.

❑ A program uses the three extension letters of COM or EXE, and a batch file, used for running programs, uses the extension letters of BAT.

Take note

You must never end a program by switching off the computer. This can leave data unsaved, so that the work you did with that program is thrown away.

2 The DOS style

Using commands

You control your computer by typing a command and then pressing the **[Enter]** key. There is a command word for each action that is possible. If there is no command word for an action, you can't do it. The list of command words is limited, and each new version of MS-DOS adds a few more.

The command word by itself may not be enough, and it often needs to be followed by other items. For example, if you type the command word **DEL** (because you want to delete a file) you have to follow this word by the name of the file you want to delete.

The file name in this example is called an *argument* for the command, and this is a word you will keep coming across.

```
BEFSETUP  MSD        33,231 08/02/93   17:17
CHKLIST   MS             27 01/02/93   15:12
CHKLIST   CPS           567 01/02/93   19:02
COMMAND   COM        54,619 30/09/93    6:20
CONFIG    SYS           464 08/12/93   17:01
CONFIG    BAK           581 11/09/93    9:11
DEFAULT   BAK         4,186 26/01/93   15:30
DEFAULT   SET         4,199 26/01/93   15:36
DEFAULT   SLT            64 26/01/93   15:36
DSUXD     386         5,741 06/12/92    6:00
HHSCAND   SYS         3,874 27/06/89   14:05
MSAU      EXE       172,134 06/12/92    6:00
MSAU      HLP        23,891 06/12/92    6:00
MSAU      INI           248 01/02/93   15:21
MSAUHELP  OUL        29,828 06/12/92    6:00
MSAUIRUS  LST        35,520 06/12/92    6:00
MSBACKDB  OUL        63,594 06/12/92    6:00
MSBACKDR  OUL        67,786 06/12/92    6:00
MSBACKFB  OUL        69,002 06/12/92    6:00
Press any key to continue . . .
```

A directory display, giving the filename, filesize, date and time for files in the C:\ drive.

This example shows the result of typing the command word DIR and pressing the **[Enter]** key. No argument has been used in this example.

1 Make sure that DOS is ready for a command – look for the prompt.

2 Make sure that you are logged to the correct drive or directory (see later).

3 Type the command word and any argument that is needed. Leave a space between the command and the argument.

4 Press the **[Enter]** key.

Take note

Throughout this book, we'll mark command words by putting them in capitals — but you don't need to type them in that way.

12

Adding to commands

☐ There must be a space between the command word and any name that follows it (the *argument*). Sometimes more than this has to be added, and the whole lot is called the command line.

☐ You use DOS commands, for example, to start a program running, to copy, delete or find files.

You can alter the effect of DIR by adding a *parameter*. In the first example below, adding /W, with a space between **DIR** and /W, gives a wide display.

The slashmark / is used so that the computer can tell that the **W** is a *parameter* and not an *argument* – you want a wide display, not a directory for drive W.

You can use both an argument and a parameter. Below is the display for **DIR A:\ /W**

Using the /W parameter fits a lot more filenames on to the screen space, making it easier for you to see how many files are on a disk or directory.

The spaces and slashes are important. There must be a space between the command word and its argument, and a space before and after each parameter. You must not mix up the forward slash / with the backslash \.

A display produced by **DIR /W**

```
Volume in drive C is HARDDISK
Volume Serial Number is 1401-311C
Directory of C:\

[ARCHIVE]      [BATS]         [BMPFILES]     [CONVERT]      [DOUBLES]
[DTP]          [EASYPC]       [EDIT]         [MSDOS]        [MSDOSBTA]
[PCXFILES]     [PP20]         [PULSAR]       [SCAN]         [SCRNGRAB]
[SKETCH3]      [STEPUP]       [TEMP]         [TIFFS]        [WINDOWS]
AUTOEXEC.BAK   AUTOEXEC.BAT   BEFSETUP.MSD   CHKLIST.MS     CHKLIST.CPS
COMMAND.COM    CONFIG.SYS     CONFIG.BAK     DEFAULT.BAK    DEFAULT.SET
DEFAULT.SLT    DSVXD.386      HHSCAND.SYS    MSAV.EXE       MSAV.HLP
MSAV.INI       MSAVHELP.OVL   MSAVIRUS.LST   MSBACKDB.OVL   MSBACKDR.OVL
MSBACKFB.OVL   MSBACKFR.OVL   MSBACKUP.RST   MSBACKUP.EXE   MSBACKUP.INI
MSBACKUP.OVL   MSBACKUP.LOG   MSBACKUP.HLP   MSBACKUP.TMP   MSBCONFG.HLF
MSBCONFG.OVL   SCANDISK.LOG   TRYIT.BAT      TRYIT          TRYIT.BAK
WINA20.386
        56 file(s)        1,333,971 bytes
                        138,895,360 bytes free
```

A display produced by **DIR A:\ /W**

```
C:\>dir a:\ /w

Volume in drive A has no label
Volume Serial Number is 0E2E-1304
Directory of A:\

ENTER.BMP      FIG1_1.BMP     FIG1_2.BMP     FRAME.BMP      ICONS.BMP
LIGHT.BMP      NOBOX.BMP      Q.BMP          WATCHIT.BMP    YESBOX.BMP
        10 file(s)         123,952 bytes
                         1,330,176 bytes free
```

Program filenames

You need to type a filename so that you can run a program. When you want to save data, like a word-processed letter, you will need to type a file name when you save it. You also need to know the filename for your data when you want to use it again.

Any filename that you use for saving your data must obey the MS-DOS rules, see right. Filenames that are unsuitable will be rejected.

If you save your data using a filename that is already in use you run the risk of losing the older file, replacing it with the new one of the same name. Some programs will warn you about this, others will not.

Here is an example of a program that requires you to type a filename.

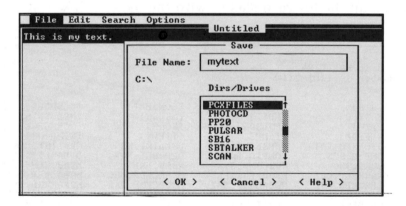

Rules

1 A filename can consist of three parts, a *path*, a *main name*, and an *extension*, separated by the colon and dot characters.

2 The main name must consist of no more than eight characters, and must start with a letter.

3 You can use letters and numbers up to the maximum total of eight.

4 You can also use the underscore and dash signs, but you should avoid any others.

5 You must not use the names of MS-DOS commands as your own filenames.

Tip

Use names that remind you what the file is for.

14

Path and extension

- ☐ The path to a file tells you where the file is. The extension tells you what kind of file it is.

- ☐ If you don't specify any path, DOS will use the drive and directory that you are logged to at the time.

- ☐ In the example, right, the path shows the drive **C:** and the directory, **EDIT**.

- ☐ The extensions DOC and TXT are often used for files of word-processor text. They are often put in automatically by word-processor programs.

The example opposite is of a program that requires you to type a filename. You can alter the drive or directory (see Section 3) by using the Dir/Drive display, and the file is saved when you type a name and select the OK box, using a mouse, or press the **[Enter]** key.

You may need to type an extension, but many programs need only the main name. In this example the directory is specified, so you don't need to type a path.

The full filename for OLDTEXT is written as:

> C:\EDIT\OLDTEXT.DOC

showing the path, the route to the directory, the main filename and the extension.

Take note

If you have to supply an extension for yourself, try to use one of the standard ones such as **TXT** or **DOC**. You must never use the extensions **EXE, COM,** or **SYS,** and you can use **BAT** only when you are saving a batch file that you have created, see later.

Finding files

Finding files is usually easy when you are using the same program to recover (open) the files as you used to save them.

The **Open** command is used almost universally by programs to mean locating and working with a data file.

Programs that supply an extension automatically when you save your data will usually list only files of that same extension (like DOC or TXT) when you open files. If you want to find files with other extensions, or with no extension at all, you will have to type the extension, or the filename.

1 Select the **Files** menu of the program.

2 From this menu, pick the **Open file** command and start it running.

3 You can then select the correct drive and directory.

4 Now you will see a list of the files, see foot of page.

5 You can now select the files that you want to use.

path

list of files with
TXT extension

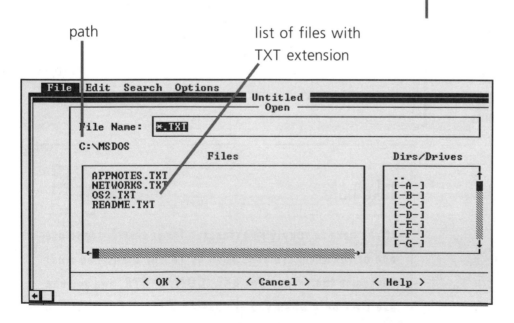

16

Basic steps

Finding files using DOS is often more long-winded.

1 You need to locate the correct directory. We'll look at that in more detail later.

2 You need to find the file in a listing. The example, right, shows a way of doing this. Once again, a full explanation will follow.

You can use whatever extensions you like this type of DIR action, such as DIR *.DOC and so on.

Finding a file of the right type is made much easier by using a variation of the DIR command. This will be explained fully later, but as an example, this is a listing produced by using **DIR *.TXT**

```
C:\MSDOS>dir *.TXT

 Volume in drive C is HARDDISK
 Volume Serial Number is 1401-311C
 Directory of C:\MSDOS

APPNOTES.TXT    NETWORKS.TXT    OS2.TXT           README.TXT
        4 file(s)          115,565 bytes
                        61,104,128 bytes free

C:\MSDOS>
```

It shows all the files that use this TXT extension, and saves a lot of time spent looking at files with other extensions, trying to single out the TXT files.

Even more saving in time can be achieved if you use DOSSHELL. This is an add-on for MS-DOS that makes it much easier to find files, but it was supplied only with MD-DOS 5.0 and 6.0, and since then has been available only on request. It's well worth requesting, and we'll refer to it on occasions throughout this book.

Tip

Know the extensions your favourite programs use.

Problems, problems

What can go wrong?

If you make a mistake in a command and press the **[Enter]** key you will see an error message such as Bad command or file name. You can either type the whole command again or you can tap the key marked **[F1]**. This key will place on screen one letter of the command line each time you press the key. You can tap the **[F1]** key until you come to the mistake, and then type the rest of the line correctly.

If you see your mistake before you press the **[Enter]** key, use the backspace key (above the down-and-left **[Enter]** key) to delete the last character that you typed. Hold the key down to delete the whole line, or tap it to delete several characters.

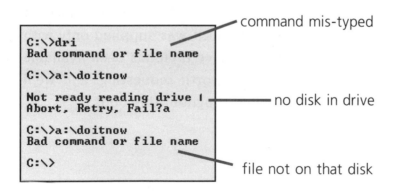

command mis-typed

no disk in drive

file not on that disk

The error message that you will see when you make a mistake should guide you to correcting the error.

Common errors

❑ You mis-type or mis-spell a command word, like **DRI** instead of **DIR**.

❑ You request an action on a floppy disk, such as **DIR A:**, but there is no disk in the drive.

❑ You try to run a program, but you don't type the path, and the program is not in the path you are logged to.

❑ You try to load a file called **MYWORD**, but you called it by the name **MYWORD.TXT** when you saved it.

❑ You try to load or run using an impossible name, like ***.***, which means any file.

More control

- The prompt was not showing when you typed the command.

- The machine has locked up because you tried to carry out an impossible command (like printing on paper with the printer switched off).

Correct use of the **CLS** and **DIR** commands can pay dividends in the shape of finding what you want very much more quickly.

When a screen becomes cluttered, you can clear it with the **CLS** command – remember that you have to press the **[Enter]** key after typing the command.

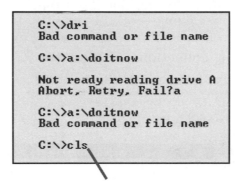

```
C:\>dri
Bad command or file name

C:\>a:\doitnow

Not ready reading drive A
Abort, Retry, Fail?a

C:\>a:\doitnow
Bad command or file name

C:\>cls
```

this will clear the screen, leaving the prompt

For example, the screen will be cluttered after a set of abortive commands, or after a **DIR** command.

Using **CLS** will clear the clutter, and if you make your **DIR** commands selective (like **DIR *.TXT**) you will get only the information that you want, unobscured by other stuff.

Take note

The commands shown in this book can be used on any version of MS-DOS from 5.0 onwards, and most of them exist also on older versions. You should aim to use as modern a version of MS-DOS as possible.

The helpful Shell

The most important commands of DOS concern copying, moving and deleting files. All these actions can be carried out very much more simply by using a program called **DOSSHELL**.

There is no space in this book to describe DOSSHELL – in detail. For further information, take a look at the book *Driving the DOSSHELL*, by Ian Sinclair from Kuma Books.

If you need to work on collections of files, the DOSSHELL will make these tasks much easier.

With DOSSHELL you can:

- ❑ display a set of directories, and the files in one directory.

- ❑ put up two such displays on the screen, and copy or move files from one to the other.

- ❑ mark a set of files and use a single command to affect all of them.

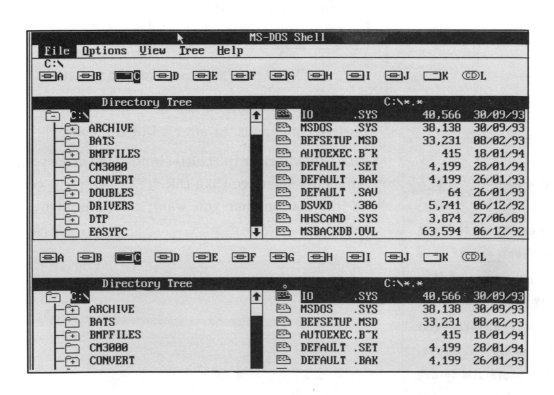

This portion of a DOSSHELLL display, illustrates two directory displays.

- display all the files on a hard disk, in alphabetical order, allowing you to find duplicates or files that you could not find otherwise.

- opt to see only the files that have the extension you are looking for,

- sort files into order of name, date of creation, extension letters and so on.

- copy, delete and move files easily with a mouse, and never need to type a filename.

- start your programs from DOSSHELL by using the mouse – no need to type program names.

A file or a set of files can be copied by using the mouse, placing the cursor over a file, holding down the mouse button and moving the cursor to the other directory. You don't need to type or memorise the file names. It is always easier to select a file rather than type its name.

In addition, DOSSHELL allows you to run programs and to hold one program suspended while you use another. DOSSHELL was supplied with MS-DOS until recently; it is now an extra.

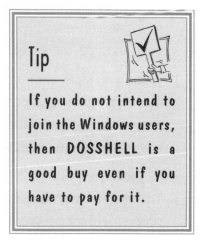

Tip

If you do not intend to join the Windows users, then **DOSSHELL** is a good buy even if you have to pay for it.

Summary

❏ Commands each consist of a single word which you have to type.

❏ Each command may need an argument to indicate what the command refers to. For example, **DIR A:** has the argument **A:** to show the drive whose listing is wanted.

❏ Many commands can also use parameters that modify the command. For example, using **/W** with **DIR** will make the listing wider, fitting more names on the screen.

❏ There must be a space between these parts of the command line.

❏ All files, whether program or data, need a file name. A full filename consists of a path, a main name, and an extension. The path is separated by a backslash, the extension by a dot.

❏ When you want to run a program, you must type its filename and possibly the path as well. You do not need to type the extension.

❏ When you save data, you will have to provide the main file name, and possibly the extension. Most programs that generate data, like word-processors, will allow you to select a path instead of typing it, and will also supply the extension automatically.

❏ The easiest way to use MS-DOS is by way of the supplementary program called DOSSHELL.

3 Drive and directory

Hard drive directories

We have seen earlier that you can change between the hard drive and a floppy drive by typing the drive letter followed by a colon and a backslash, such as:

    A:\   or   C:\

followed by pressing [Enter].

The hard drive can store very much more than can be stored on a floppy disk; it might have the storage capacity of a hundred or more floppies.

This makes it important to have some way of subdividing the space, because otherwise you might be looking for a filename in a set of 4,000 or more files. This way is the use of directories.

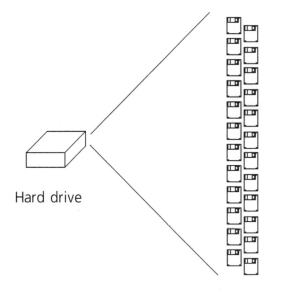

Hard drive

equivalent
floppies

You can think of a hard disk as a large set of floppies, each one of which you can use just by typing its name.

❑ The use of directories allows files to be stored in groups, such as all text files in one directory.

❑ The DIR command can be applied to a directory rather than to the whole disk.

❑ You can have two files stored using the same filename, as long as they are in different directories.

❑ You can normally store only 128 files on a disk, but you can put as many files as you like in a directory – as long as they do not exceed the storage capacity of the hard disk.

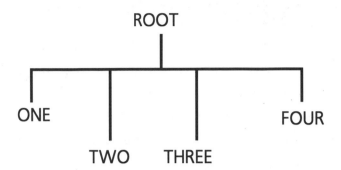

The main directory is called the root – it is the directory
we use on any disk where no other directories have been
created.

In a diagram, we can show the root directory as if it were
the ancestor of all others – the words parent and child
are often used of directories.

The MS-DOS **DIR** command does not show a diagram like
this – you cannot see the directory structure.

When you use a DIR command on the hard drive root
(usually C:\) you get a display where the names of other
directories are shown in square brackets.

```
Volume in drive C is HARDDISK
Volume Serial Number is 1401-311C
Directory of C:\

[ARCHIVE]       [BATS]          [BMPFILES]      [CM3000]        [CONVERT]
[DOUBLES]       [DRIVERS]       [DTP]           [EASYPC]        [EDIT]
[ENCARTA]       [GRPHUTIL]      [ICONS]         [LIBRIS]        [MMWA]
[MONOLOGW]      [MSDOS]         [MSDOSBTA]      [MUSICSYS]      [NGME]
[PANA]          [PCXFILES]      [PHOTOCD]       [PP20]          [PULSAR]
[SB16]          [SBTALKER]      [SCAN]          [SCRNGRAB]      [STEPUP]
[TEMP]          [TEST]          [TIFFS]         [WINDOWS]       [WSKETCH]
AUTOEXEC.B~K    AUTOEXEC.BAK    AUTOEXEC.OLD    AUTOEXEC.INB    AUTOEXEC.BAT
BEFSETUP.MSD    CHKLIST.MS      CHKLIST.CPS     COMMAND.COM     CONFIG.B~K
CONFIG.INB      CONFIG.SYS      CONFIG.BAK      CSAMP.EXE       DEFAULT.SET
DEFAULT.BAK     DEFAULT.SAV     DEFAULT.SLT     DSUXD.386       HHSCAND.SYS
```

The MS-DOS DIR display, above, shows the main directories with their names placed
between square brackets. No sub-directories are shown – you cannot see in this
listing any directories of ARCHIVE, for example.

Root and branch

You can have directories that branch from other directories; these are called sub-directories. In the diagram, the sub-directory called **twoone** is a child of **ONE**, and **ONE** is a child of the **root**. The path to **twoone** is written as:

C:\ONE\TWOONE

- going from the root through the parent.

When you type a path like this, you can either start at some directory along the path, or from the root. The backslash (\) is used to mean the root when a path starts with a backslash.

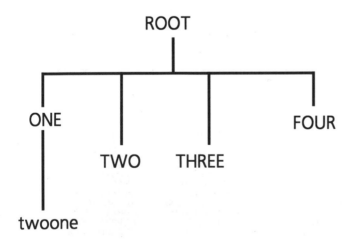

Uses

❑ You can keep the data files that belong to a program in a separate sub-directory, not in the same directory as houses the program.

❑ You can create several sub-directories of a directory that contains a program, so that you can separate different types of data files (like letters, memos, proposals, CVs and so on).

❑ You can use separate sub-directories to hold files that have the same filename without one file replacing the others of the same name.

26

Names and extensions

Directories and sub-directories are identified by name. You can use a name that follows the same rules as a filename, using only letters and numerals with no punctuation marks and no special characters except for the underscore.

You can also use an extension for a directory name if you want; for example, MYWRITE.WRK is a valid name with its three-letter extension. For most purposes this is not necessary, and it is more to type in a path name. For some purposes, though, it can be a useful way of allowing you to use eleven letters in a directory name.

Take note

There are limits. You are allowed to use only as many layers of directory and sub-directory as would take 64 characters to type in a path. That's equivalent to eight-deep, and most of us have never gone more than three-deep.

Changing directory

You often need to change directory. The program you want to run may be in another directory, or the data you want to use is in another directory.

The **CD** command is used for this purpose – the name is a reminder of the action **C**hange **D**irectory.

A CD command has to be followed by a path to the directory you want. How this path is written depends on what directory you are currently using – see the diagram below.

This illustrates some directories and sub-directories, with a few example paths from one to another.

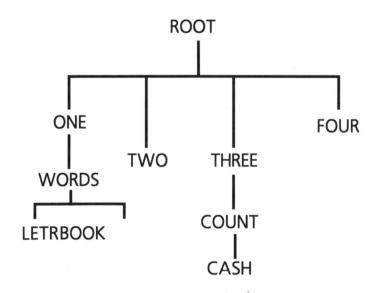

From WORDS to LETR: **CD LETR**
From WORDS to ONE: **CD .. (or CD \ONE)**
From WORDS to COUNT: **CD\THREE\COUNT**
From THREE to CASH: **CD COUNT\CASH**

Rules

- To go to a directory in the same line below the one you are in, use **CD** followed by the path, with no backslash to start.

  Example:

  CD COUNT\CASH

- To go to a directory one step back, use **CD..** (two dots).

- To go to the root directory, use

  **CD ** \ +/- space

  with only the backslash following **CD**.

- If the directory is in another branch, use **CD ** to get back to the root, and type the path from there.

  Example:

  CD:\THREE\COUNT

- You must use the back-slash sign between path names.

- MS-DOS shows the directories as names in square brackets. If you used **CD \ONE** in the previous example you would see [WORDS] in square brackets – but you would not see LETR or BOOK unless you logged on to WORDS and used **DIR**.

- Finding your way around directories means using **CD** and **DIR** commands in turn until you get to the one you want.

change to dtp directory

get a directory list

there is a directory called PUB

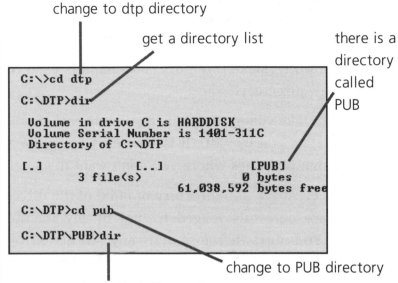

```
C:\>cd dtp

C:\DTP>dir

 Volume in drive C is HARDDISK
 Volume Serial Number is 1401-311C
 Directory of C:\DTP

[.]              [..]              [PUB]
        3 file(s)               0 bytes
                       61,038,592 bytes free

C:\DTP>cd pub

C:\DTP\PUB>dir
```

change to PUB directory

DIR again to find files and any other sub-directories.

Finding sub-directories is a tedious process when you use MS-DOS directly – see the following pages for easier methods of finding your way around directories.

Finding the way is even more difficult if you have not set up MS-DOS to show the main directories grouped together. In the next example, the directories are scattered through the listing rather than being placed at the start.

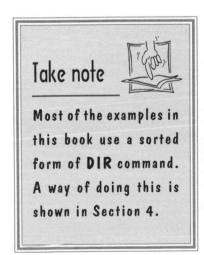

Take note

Most of the examples in this book use a sorted form of **DIR** command. A way of doing this is shown in Section 4.

```
Directory of C:\

[BATS]          BEFSETUP.MSD    AUTOEXEC.B~K    [CONVERT]
DEFAULT.BAK     DEFAULT.SAV     DSVXD.386       [DTP]
HHSCAND.SYS     MSBACKDB.OVL    MSBACKDR.OVL    MSBACKFB.OVL
MSBACKUP.RST    MSBACKUP.EXE    MSBACKUP.INI    MSBACKUP.OVL
MSBACKUP.HLP    MSBACKUP.TMP    MSBCONFG.HLP    MSBCONFG.OVL
[BMPFILES]      [EASYPC]        AUTOEXEC.BAK    CONFIG.B~K
[STEPUP]        [PCXFILES]      [SCAN]          [SCRNGRAB]
[TEMP]          [TIFFS]         [WSKETCH]       WINA20.386
SCANDISK.LOG    [ARCHIVE]       COMMAND.COM     MSAV.EXE
AUTOEXEC.OLD    [SB16]          MSAV.HLP        MSAVHELP.OVL
CHKLIST.MS      MSAV.INI        CHKLIST.CPS     DEFAULT.SLT
CONFIG.INB      TRYIT.BAT       AUTOEXEC.INB    AUTOEXEC.BAT
[NGME]          [TEST]          [PP20]          [SBTALKER]
CONFIG.SYS      [LIBRIS]        [MONOLOGW]      [PHOTOCD]
TMP9            [ICONS]         [DRIVERS]       [MUSICSYS]
[CM3000]        README          ST.EXE          CSAMP.EXE
REGISTER.DOC    TECH.DOC        RELEASE.DOC     REGISTER.FRM
ST.ILB          STA0.ILB        ST02.ILB        ST03.ILB
[GRPHUTIL]      TMP86           CONFIG.BAK
        93 file(s)      1,530,756 bytes
                       61,022,208 bytes free
```

Creating a directory

The **MD** or **MDIR** (Make Directory) command is used to create a new directory.

You need to take some care over the directory that you log on to when you use MD. It is very easy to create a directory that branches where you don't want it.

MD always creates a sub-directory or child of the directory you are currently logged to, not of any remote directory. You must therefore start any MD action by logging on to the directory that you want to be the parent.

The most certain way is to draw out the part of the tree diagram that shows where you want the new directory to appear. This will remind you of which directory you need to be logged to when you use the MD command.

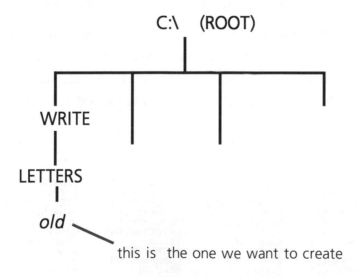

this is the one we want to create

MS-DOS Steps

```
CD \WRITE\LETTERS [Enter]
MD old [Enter]
```

The directory is now ready.

Basic steps

1 Decide where you want the directory. Is it to branch from the root or from another directory?

2 Log on to the root or the directory from which your new directory will branch.

3 Type the command **MD** and follow it with a space then the name of the new directory.

4 Press [Enter] to create the directory.

5 Check with a tree diagram (or part of a tree diagram) that the directory is in the right place.

You can create directories on floppy disks as well as on the hard drive. There are several reasons for doing this:

❑ You might want to save a large number of small files. If you used the root directory you would be limited to 128 files, even if these took up only 100 Kbyte on a 1.4 Mbyte disk

❑ You might want to save two sets of files, each of which had files with identical names, like README.TXT.

❑ Using directories on a floppy is a safeguard against deleting every-thing with a **DEL *.*** command. If you use floppies for essential backups this is worth noting.

Always check the tree after creating a directory and if you get it wrong, delete the directory using RD before you start to fill it with files. (See Section 8.)

As always, you should keep an up-to-date copy of your directory tree each time you start to create a directory, and you should add in the new directory once it has been created.

The use of directories became necessary when hard disks were first fitted to PC machines. Modern floppy disks have an amount of space that is quite large compared to the old-style floppies, and in some cases you need to use directories on floppies.

Floppies used to distribute programs are often divided into directories, particularly if a large number of small files are included. You should not alter the directory structure of such a floppy, because this will probably make it unusable. The SETUP or INSTALL program on distribution disks usually contains commands that copy files from directories on the floppy, and any change can make these actions impossible, leaving you with no backup of your program.

DOSSHELL directories

As usual, DOSSHELL users get the best of it - they can see the tree as they select the New Directory option.

Creating a new directory with DOSSHELL is simple, and you can see what you are doing - the illustration below is a composite of two parts of the screen.

The cursor is placed on the parent directory, and the mouse is used to activate the **Create Directory** menu item, see the steps described, right. You are asked for a directory name and when the action is complete you will see the new directory in place on the tree diagram.

❑ **Mouse**

1 Click on the directory that is to be the parent from which the new directory will branch.

2 Click on the **Files** menu and select **New Directory**.

3 Fill in the name of the new directory, see opposite. This will now be created and you will see the directory tree display alter to show the new directory.

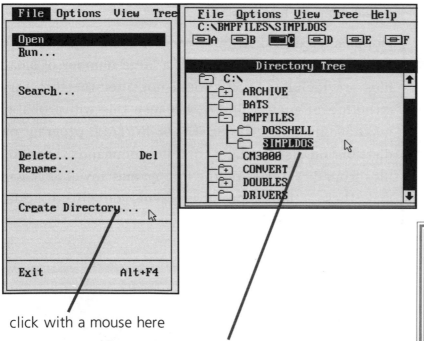

click with a mouse here

to make a sub-directory of this

Take note

You can use any name for a directory, subject to the usual filename rules, and provided it is not the same as that of the parent directory.

Basic steps

❏ Keys

1 Press the [Alt] key and release it. You will see the menu items highlighted.

2 Now press the [F] key for the **File** menu. You will see the letter **e** in **Create Directory** highlighted.

3 Press the [E] key, and you will see the form that asks you to fill in the name for the new directory.

The illustration shows the DOSSHELL form that appears when you create a new directory.

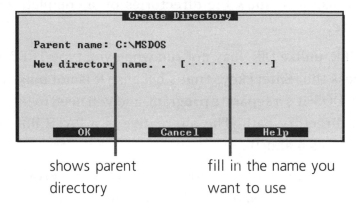

shows parent
directory

fill in the name you
want to use

The convenience that DOSSHELL offers in terms of working with directories, particularly for creating and deleting directories, makes its use very desirable if you are using DOS programs.

Tip

A directory name can have an extension. You can, for example, create a directory with a name such as **TEXTFILE.NEW**, which allows you eleven letters (and the dot). Do remember that you might find this more tedious to type when you are using **CD** commands.

Finding directories

There is a command called TREE which will give a display that is more useful, but the diagram is very large when you use it to show the directories of a complete hard drive.

TREE, unlike DIR, may not run when you type **TREE** and press the **[Enter]** key. That's because it is not built in to MS-DOS; it's a separate program, and you need to include its directory path. The alternative is a PATH line, see Sections 4 and 16.

The TREE command shows the root as a vertical line down the left hand side. This is only a fraction of the TREE diagram for a hard disk – it is more useful when it is printed on paper.

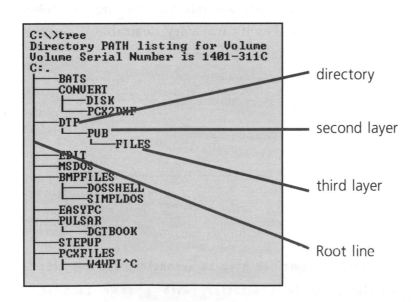

With a printed TREE diagram you can find the path to any directory quickly and easily. You can print TREEs that also show files, but these are often too bulky to be useful.

1 Find where the TREE.COM program is located. This will usually be in a directory called MSDOS or DOS, depending on how your machine is set up.

2 Log on to this directory and type

   TREE C:

   then press **[Enter]**.

3 The screen is likely to scroll too quickly for you to read the listing easily.

4 Put your printer on line and loaded with paper.

5 Type the command:

   TREE   C:\ > PRN

   and press **[Enter]**. This will print out the listing on paper if the printer is correctly set up.

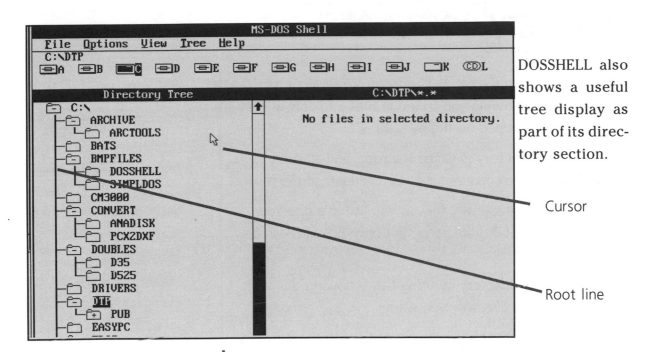

DOSSHELL also shows a useful tree display as part of its directory section.

Cursor

Root line

- ❏ If you are in any doubt about a CD command, use CD\ to start from the root directory, as this will always work.

- ❏ Using meaningful names like MONEY, WORDS, DRAWINGS and so on for main directories help you to find groups of sub-directories for these actions.

This is a display that is more usable on the screen, because it does not scroll down by itself. You can scroll it for yourself by using the mouse (dragging the scrollbars) or the keys.

You will avoid a lot of frustration if you know your directory tree, because you can waste a lot of time in alternate CD and DIR commands looking for the correct directory to use.

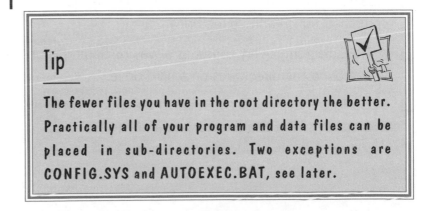

Tip

The fewer files you have in the root directory the better. Practically all of your program and data files can be placed in sub-directories. Two exceptions are CONFIG.SYS and AUTOEXEC.BAT, see later.

Summary

❑ Directories are the MS-DOS way of organising a hard disk drive, allowing you to group files into sets as they would be grouped on floppy disks.

❑ The main directory is called the **root**, and all other directories are subdirectories (or children) of the root.

❑ You can store as many files as you like in a directory (subject to total disk space), but only 128 files can be stored in the root.

❑ You change directory by using **CD**, following this with a path to the directory you want.

❑ Remember the useful short-cut of **CD..** to the previous (parent) directory.

❑ Before you create a new directory, draw a tree diagram to show where the new directory will go - perhaps as a subdirectory of an existing one.

❑ You can then log to this parent directory and use **MD** to create the new sub-directory. Use a Tree display to check that it is where it should be.

❑ A directory name can use an extension of up to three letters just like any filename.

❑ **DOSSHELL** is much more convenient than the **MD** command for creating directories .

❑ A **TREE** diagram is very useful as a way of finding your way around the directories on a hard drive.

❑ **DOSSHELL** is even easier for seeing the Tree structure and moving from one directory to another.

4 Running a program

Using names and paths

A program file will be distinguished from other files, such as your data file, by its extension name, which will be COM or EXE. You do not need to type that part of the name when you run the program.

Running a program is the most important MS-DOS action, because running programs is what you bought the computer for in the first place.

As always, you must spell the name of the program absolutely correctly, and the same goes for each stage in the path. 100% correct is just about good enough.

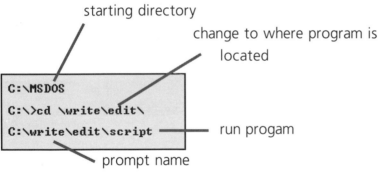

starting directory

change to where program is located

```
C:\MSDOS
C:\>cd \write\edit\
C:\write\edit\script
```

run progam

prompt name

program runs, returns to C:\WRITE\EDIT directory

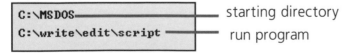

```
C:\MSDOS
C:\write\edit\script
```

starting directory

run program

program runs, return to C:\MSDOS directory

❏ **To run a program**

1 Locate the program file; for example if it was in the directory:

C:\WRITE\EDIT

2 EITHER:

a Log to this directory by using:

CD \WRITE\EDIT

then run the program by typing its name and pressing **[Enter]**.

OR

b Type the program name at the end of the path, and press **[Enter]**. For example, if the program is called SCRIPT.EXE, you would type:

\WRITE\EDIT\SCRIPT

- For many users, using a full path name can be a source of endless errors, because if there are several names in the path, the chances of mistyping are increased.

- The remedy is to make use of a batch file, which is just the command line typed perfectly and saved as a file with a BAT extension. See Section 12 for details of this way of preserving your sanity.

The two methods of running a program differ in an important way. The first starts from the directory that the program is in and returns there after the program ends. The second can start from any directory, and will return to that directory after the program ends.

For many purposes, this second option is more useful.

You cannot run a program if you do not know what directory it is in, because you must either log on to that directory, or use its name in the path portion of the command. Either way, if you are using a command that is in a remote sub-directory, you have a lot of typing to do.

Using DOSSHELL is another way around this problem, because you do not then need to be able to type any names, just select what you want. It's a bit like multiple-choice questions – it take a lot of effort to get it wrong.

Take note

When the program ends you will be returned to the directory you were logged on to. In the first example, this will be the directory that contained the program. In the second example, it will be where you started.

DOS commands

The MS-DOS commands are of two types, internal and external.

The internal commands are available to you as long as the command prompt is showing.

The external commands, such as TREE, are programs held on the disk, and they have to be run like any other programs, by using a path as noted earlier.

Fortunately, there is a way of making external commands run in much the same way as internal commands, no matter what directory you happen to be using. The key to this is to use PATH as a command to indicate the directories that you want DOS to use if no other information is supplied.

```
C:\SB16\SB16SET /M:220 /UOC:220 /CD:220 /MIDI:220
PATH C:\MSDOS:C:\:C:\WINDOWS:C:\BATS:C:\monologw
```

Any program in these directories will run like an MS-DOS internal program.

The directories are:

C:\MSDOS .... where MSDOS files are stored
C:\ .... the root
C:\WINDOWS .... Windows directory
C:\BATS .... batch files directory
C:\MONOLOGW .... directory for talking reader

Internal commands

CD – change directory

CLS – clear screen

COPY – copy files

DATE – set date

DEL – delete file

DIR – show listing

MD – create directory

PATH – list preferred
paths

PROMPT – change
prompt

REN – rename file

RD – remove directory

SET – set variables

TIME – set time

TYPE – show data on
screen

VER – show MS-DOS
version

VOL – show disk name

Basic steps

1 Type **PATH** and a space.

2 Now type the **C:** root directory name, followed by a semicolon.

3 Now type another path to a directory you want to use, such as **C:\MSDOS** or **C:\DOS**.

4 Place a semicolon before each new directory name.

5 Continue for all the directories that you want to include.

The next step is how to use a PATH line. You could type it at any time, but if the line is written into the AUTOEXEC.BAT file, it will be run automatically each time the computer is booted. See Section 13 for details of AUTOEXEC.BAT.

Setting up a PATH line

The listing on the previous page is part of one obtained by using the command:

TYPE C:\AUTOEXEC.BAT

It shows the PATH command line that sets up directories to be searched when you type a program name without specifying a directory path.

The PATH command contains a list of directory paths. Any program in these directories will run like an internal command, regardless of the directory you are using.

You need only a few directories in a PATH line, because if your hard disk is correctly organised all the MS-DOS external commands (utilities) are in one directory called C:\MSDOS or C:\DOS.

Some well-known external commands are:

CHKDSK	DBLSPACE	DEFRAG	DELTREE
DISKCOMP	DISKCOPY	DOSHELP	DOSKEY
DOSSHELL	EDIT	EXPAND	FC
FIND	FORMAT	HELP	KEYB
LABEL	MEM	MEMMAKER	MODE
MORE	MOVE	MSAV	MSBACKUP
MSD	PRINT	SHARE	SORT
TREE	UNDELETE	UNFORMAT	VERIFY
VSAFEXCOPY			

Using parameters

Parameters for programs are short coded instructions that alter the way that the program works.

For example, you might have a word-processor that did not work well with a monochrome screen unless you added a parameter to make it display in black and white. For example, if the program is called **SCRIPT**, you might type the command as:

> SCRIPT /BW

- with the **/BW** being the parameter that forces the program to work in this way.

directory

program name

parameters

```
C:\SB16\SB16SET /M:220 /VOC:220 /CD:220 /MIDI:220 /LINE:220 /TREBLE:0
```

Notes

1 Read the program manual to find what parameters can be used and how to use them. Some MS-DOS commands, such as DIR, can take parameters; others can not.

2 Programs that take parameters often allow you to use more than one, in which case they must be separated, usually by slashes or spaces.

3 Some programs allow you to use a filename as a parameter. When the program runs, that filename will be used as the data file. If the file does not exist, it will be created.

Feed Me!

- Using arguments and/or parameters is one way of feeding data into a program.

- There is another way that uses the command word SET, see the example on the right. This has to run before any program that will use its information, and it is followed by parameters. These are available until the computer is switched off – they do not vanish when the program ends.

- SET lines would normally be placed in the AUTOEXEC.BAT file, see later.

Some programs require a slash placed before each parameter, other simply require a space. This is information that you have to get from the manual for the program (so you do have to read it).

The example on the previous page shows a program name followed by six parameters. This can be very tedious to type each time you need it, and MS-DOS allows for automation of such examples, see Section 15.

SET example:

```
SET BLASTER=A220 I5 D1 H5 P330 T6
SET SOUND=C:\SB16


set dircmd=/w/p/o:gn
set temp=c:\temp
```

The general form is SET name=parameter

There must be no space either side of the equals sign. The names that you use in SET lines are usually required by specific programs. In the example above, **BLASTER** and **SOUND** are needed for the sound board, **dircmd** is needed for DIR, and **temp** is used by a large number of different programs.

Different DIRs

The DIR command is probably the one you will use most of all, so it is one that you should learn to use properly.

The simple DIR produces a detailed listing of the files and sub-directories, showing the sizes of files and the dates and times that they were last changed. Though all very interesting, it is sometimes too much.

Each file takes one line on the screen, but there are only 25 lines on a screen and you very often have more than 25 files in one directory. As a result, a simple DIR will very often produce a listing that scrolls up and off the top of the screen before you can read it. The question is, what can we do to DIR so that we can see the list properly.

There are two parameters that will solve the problem in different ways /W for Wide and /P for Pause. We met the Wide option earlier.

```
FIG6_3      PCX     14316 28/03/94   12:28
FIG7_1      PCX      6227 28/03/94   12:28
FIG7_2      PCX      4583 08/03/94   14:59
FIG7_3      PCX      1703 28/03/94   12:29
FIG7_4      PCX      2043 28/03/94   12:29
FIG8_1      PCX      4268 28/03/94   12:30
FIG8_10     PCX      3287 30/03/94    0:08
FIG8_11     PCX      3503 30/03/94    0:09
FIG8_2      PCX     25039 08/03/94   16:35
FIG8_3      PCX      2795 28/03/94   12:31
FIG8_4      PCX      4407 28/03/94   12:32
FIG8_5      PCX      2350 28/03/94   12:32
FIG8_6      PCX      4744 28/03/94   12:33
FIG8_7      PCX      8927 28/03/94   12:33
FIG8_8      PCX      8087 29/03/94   23:19
FIG8_9      PCX      2839 28/03/94   12:35
FIG9_1      PCX      6625 28/03/94   12:35
FIG9_2      PCX      6755 28/03/94   12:36
FIG9_3      PCX      8526 28/03/94   12:36
FIG8_12     PCX      1642 30/03/94    0:07
        101 file(s)      643033 bytes
                       32286720 bytes free
```

A listing from a simple DIR – sometimes called a narrow DIR, to distinguish it from the Wide variety.

Wide and Pause

/W makes DIR produce a Wide listing – filenames are displayed, without their size and date information, across the width of the screen. For example:

DIR \W

will display all the files in the current directory.

/P makes **DIR** Pause at the end of each screenful. When you press any key, the screen scrolls up and pauses at the end of the next screenful. For example:

DIR C:\MSDOS /P

will give a full listing of the files in a directory called MSDOS, one screenful at a time.

Sorted lists

/O sets a sorting order. It must be followed by a colon and a letter to show which order. A minus sign before the letter reverses its effect.

Key ones are:

/O:N alphabetical by name

/O:D date, earliest first

/O:S size, smallest first

/O:-S size, largest first

/O:G directories before files

```
Directory of  C:\SIMPLDOS\PIX.PCX
.               <DIR>     10/04/94    23:23
..              <DIR>     10/04/94    23:23
FIG1_1    PCX      5819  21/03/94    16:54
FIG1_2    PCX      1667  21/03/94    16:54
FIG1_3    PCX      1299  21/03/94    16:54
FIG1_4    PCX      7780  26/03/94    12:43
FIG1_5    PCX      2213  26/03/94    12:45
FIG1_6    PCX      9200  26/03/94    12:46
FIG1_7    PCX      3186  21/03/94    16:56
FIG1_8    PCX      7072  26/03/94    13:33
FIG1_9    PCX      8147  26/03/94    12:48
FIG10_1   PCX      6484  12/04/94    23:08
FIG10_2   PCX      8214  13/04/94     0:30
FIG10_3   PCX      6752  09/03/94    16:49
FIG10_4   PCX      4694  12/04/94    23:08
FIG10_5   PCX      5203  12/04/94    23:09
FIG10_6   PCX      9747  12/04/94    23:09
FIG11_1   PCX      6742  09/03/94    20:53
FIG11_2   PCX     12030  12/04/94    23:10
Press any key to continue . . .
```

Above: A listing from **DIR /P**. This has another 6 screensful to go. Pressing any key will display the next set.

Below: Part of a listing from **DIR /W**. At 5-columns wide, over 100 filenames can be displayed on screen this way.

```
FIG3_9.PCX     FIG4_1.PCX     FIG4_2.PCX     FIG4_3.PCX     FIG4_4.PCX
FIG5_1.PCX     FIG5_2.PCX     FIG5_3.PCX     FIG5_4.PCX     FIG5_5.PCX
FIG5_6.PCX     FIG5_7.PCX     FIG5_8.PCX     FIG5_9.PCX     FIG6_1.PCX
FIG6_2.PCX     FIG6_3.PCX     FIG7_1.PCX     FIG7_2.PCX     FIG7_3.PCX
FIG7_4.PCX     FIG8_1.PCX     FIG8_10.PCX    FIG8_11.PCX    FIG8_2.PCX
FIG8_3.PCX     FIG8_4.PCX     FIG8_5.PCX     FIG8_6.PCX     FIG8_7.PCX
FIG8_8.PCX     FIG8_9.PCX     FIG9_1.PCX     FIG9_2.PCX     FIG9_3.PCX
FIG8_12.PCX    FIG4_5.PCX
       102 file(s)      670892 bytes
                     32258048 bytes free
```

Take note

The display style produced by **DIR** can be changed by setting the dircmd variable in your **AUTOEXEC.BAT** file. See Section 13.

Summary

❏ A program file is recognised by its extension letters, which are **COM** or **EXE**.

❏ A program is run by typing its filename (without the COM or EXE portion) and pressing **[Enter]**.

❏ If you are not logged on to the directory where the program is stored you must either log on to that directory before typing the program name, or include the path in the program name.

❏ The program name and (if used) the path, must be spelled and typed perfectly. Do not confuse the backslash with the forward slash. Remember that if you hit the backslash key with the **[Shift]** key down you will get the | character, which is not the same as a backslash.

❏ Some programs can take arguments and/or parameters following the filename. These are not always needed, but if they are, they have to be separated correctly from the program name and from each other. The usual separators are the forward slash (/) or a space.

❏ **DIR** can take the parameters **/W**, **/P** and **/O** to change the style of the listing display.

❏ The **SET** command can also be used to convey information to a program that runs later. Whatever is SET remains available until the machine is switched off (unless it is countermanded).

5 Formatting

FORMATting floppies

FORMAT is an important MS-DOS command that is used to format floppy disks, usually new blank disks.

Before they can be used, they must be recorded to mark out the way that the PC machine will store data on them.

This process of formatting marks out the tracks on the disk, and divides each track into sectors, each of which can store 512 bytes of data. In addition, a directory file is prepared to hold the names (up to 128) of the files you will store on the disk.

The Basic Steps given here apply to modern PCs with 1.4Mb floppy drives.

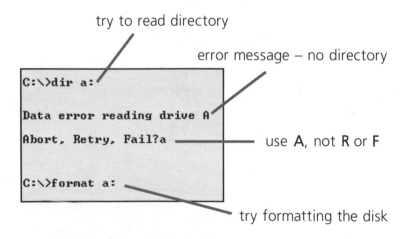

try to read directory

error message – no directory

use **A**, not **R** or **F**

try formatting the disk

If you now see the disk being formatted, you know there is nothing wrong with the drive or the computer. You have simply tried to read an unformatted disk.

1 Place the unformatted disk into the A: drive.

2 Make sure you are logged on to the hard drive, usually C:\

3 Make sure you have access to the MSDOS files - either by logging on to the directory where they are held or by the use of a PATH command.

4 If the disk is a High Density, 1.4Mb, just type

FORMAT A:

If it is a Double Density, 720Kb disk, type

FORMAT A: \F:720

Do not try to format a 720 KB disk as 1.44 MB. You can format a 1.44 MB disk as 720 KB if you need to.

5 You will be asked to put a disk in the drive and press **[Enter]**. Do it.

6 Formatting is a fairly slow operation. You will see the progress of a format displayed as a percentage.

7 When the formatting is finished, you will be asked if you want to format another. Answer Y or N. If you answer Y you will then be asked to insert another blank disk into the drive.

8 You can format a disk that has been formatted and used. Formatting will remove any files that were on the disk.

You will get an error message if you work with an unformatted disk, or one that has been formatted on a different type of machine such as an Apple Mac. A disk that has been formatted on a PC machine will work with any other PC machine, regardless of manufacturer.

Volume Labels

You do not need to fill in a Label Name unless you want to - it can be convenient if you want to reserve disks for special purposes.

The Label Name, or Volume Label, is a name that you can type to identify your disk. If you use a Label name, it will appear each time you use a DIR command to see the files on the disk. This is useful if your floppy disks are used to retain data for a long time (as they usually are).

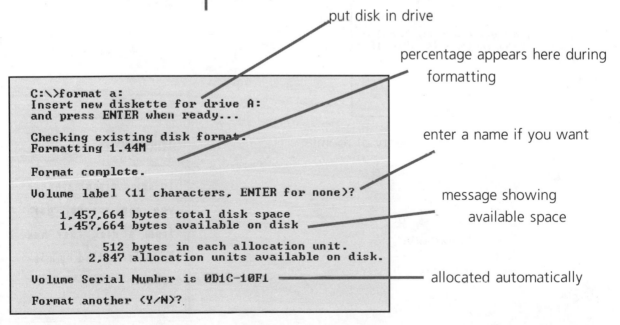

put disk in drive

percentage appears here during formatting

enter a name if you want

message showing available space

allocated automatically

```
C:\>format a:
Insert new diskette for drive A:
and press ENTER when ready...

Checking existing disk format.
Formatting 1.44M

Format complete.

Volume label (11 characters, ENTER for none)?

    1,457,664 bytes total disk space
    1,457,664 bytes available on disk

        512 bytes in each allocation unit.
      2,847 allocation units available on disk.

Volume Serial Number is 0D1C-10F1

Format another (Y/N)?
```

Numbers and system

The serial number for a newly-formatted floppy is allocated by the computer - it is a sort of random password, but you do not need to keep a record of it unless you want to be able to identify the disks. Using a sticky label is more convenient!

Remember that if you try to use a floppy disk that has not been formatted you will get an error message - it often takes some time before the message is delivered.

When you command a DIR of a formatted disk that has no files recorded, this is the screen display. Older versions of DOS showed the space available.

this disk is formatted but not yet used for files

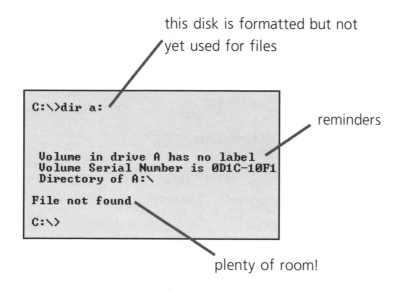

```
C:\>dir a:


 Volume in drive A has no label
 Volume Serial Number is 0D1C-10F1
 Directory of A:\

File not found

C:\>
```

reminders

plenty of room!

Dodgy disk?

❏ If you have any doubts about a floppy disk, save whatever files you can from it on to a reliable floppy, and re-format the dubious one.

❏ If it seems to take several shots at one track, then throw it away before you commit any more effort to it.

❏ Disks are cheap, your time is not.

Take note

In some circumstances you can recover data from a disk that has been formatted by mistake.

Basic steps

1 Put a blank disk in drive A:.

2 Type the FORMAT command, adding the parameter /S at the end to give

FORMAT A: /S

3 After formatting, you will see a message about copying the system files.

❑ When you use **DIR** on a System disk the only file name shown is COMMAND.COM.

❑ There are two *hidden* files, MSDOS.SYS and IO.SYS which are not shown in the listing.

This disk had been formatted by MS-DOS 6.2 and data can be recovered after a FORMAT

A System floppy is one that has System files recorded on it, usually at the time when the floppy is formatted. The System files are the files of MS-DOS that are used when the computer is booted.

You can insert a System Floppy in the drive, switch on the computer, and boot up MS-DOS from the floppy rather than from the hard drive.

Some computers insist on this process, some use the hard drive unless there is a floppy in the A: drive, others totally ignore the floppy drive and always boot from the hard drive. You can usually set up the computer yourself for any one of these options - see the computer manual entry on setting up CMOS RAM.

command uses /S

System files are copied

Space used for MS-DOS

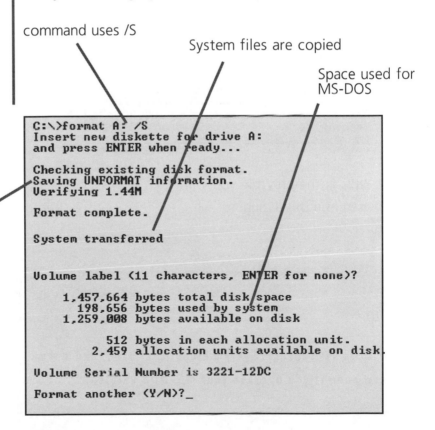

```
C:\>format A: /S
Insert new diskette for drive A:
and press ENTER when ready...

Checking existing disk format.
Saving UNFORMAT information.
Verifying 1.44M

Format complete.

System transferred

Volume label (11 characters, ENTER for none)?

    1,457,664 bytes total disk space
      198,656 bytes used by system
    1,259,008 bytes available on disk

          512 bytes in each allocation unit.
        2,459 allocation units available on disk.

Volume Serial Number is 3221-12DC

Format another (Y/N)?_
```

The main system files

The COMMAND.COM file is one that you can see in a listing of a newly-formatted System disk. This contains the MS-DOS commands, and each version of MS-DOS uses a different version of the COMMAND.COM file.

If you use a different version of the file COMMAND.COM with your system, you will get an error message - all the files of MS-DOS must be from the same version.

this disk was formatted with FORMAT A: /S

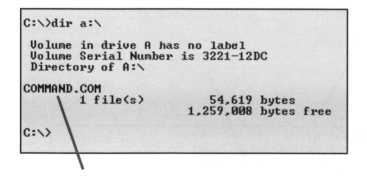

```
C:\>dir a:\

 Volume in drive A has no label
 Volume Serial Number is 3221-12DC
 Directory of A:\

COMMAND.COM
        1 file(s)              54,619 bytes
                           1,259,008 bytes free

C:\>
```

this is the only file you will
see in a DIR listing

COMMAND.COM which contains the internal MS-DOS commands.

IO.SYS which controls the way that programs use the computers keyboard, mouse, screen, printer and all other inputs and outputs.

MSDOS.SYS which sees to all the other control actions .

❏ If your computer uses the disk **Doublespace** utility, your System disks will also contain a file called DBLSPACE.BIN.

Tip

Always have several System Floppies at hand, and make new ones if you upgrade your MS-DOS version.

Seeing hidden files

- You can make **DIR**, show two of the System files. Adding the parameter **/a:sh** will show only the hidden and system files (not the ordinary files)

- A **DOSSHELL** display can reveal ordinary files, system and hidden files, and one that DIR cannot show.

  DOUBLESPACE.BIN is used with the MS-DOS version 6.2 utility DBLSPACE to compress files on the hard drive, allowing you to save more files on the drive.

The normal DIR used on a System floppy shows only the COMMAND.COM file, but there are two other files also present. They are hidden so that you do not delete them by accident - deleting these files makes the disk unusable as a System disk.

these parameters make DIR show system and hidden files only

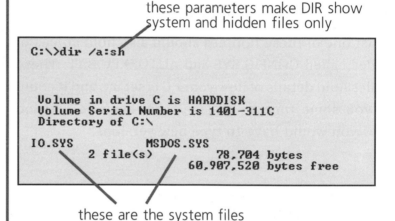

these are the system files

Using **DIR A: /a:sh** will allow DIR to display only these system or hidden files, not the others.

DOSSHELL can show more:

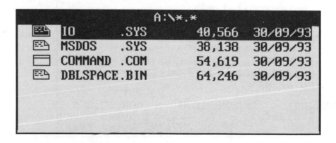

As usual, DOSSHELL make it a lot easier to see everything that is on a disk

Backing up your system

And why...

Make several of these System floppies as soon as you set up your computer system, and each time you change to a new version of MS-DOS.

These floppies are your System backup and are valuable. Label them carefully and put them in a cool place where they will not suffer from condensation. They should also be kept well away from magnets.

At least one of these floppies should also hold copies of the files called CONFIG.SYS and AUTOEXEC.BAT. These two files hold details of how your PC is set up, and it could take you some time to replace them because with no copies you would have to type new versions.

1 Some day you will have problems with your hard drive, and the computer will not boot from it. With a System disk you can boot from drive A: .

2 If your PC picks up a virus from a rogue floppy or from a file received by modem, your first step to recovery is to boot from one of your System floppies, which should be virus-free.

3 Some versions of DOS will only allow a System floppy to be made from an existing System floppy.

❏ Modern DOS versions allow you to make a System Floppy from the files on the hard disk.

start with the C:\> prompt showing, and a System disk in the A: drive

copy this file

and this one

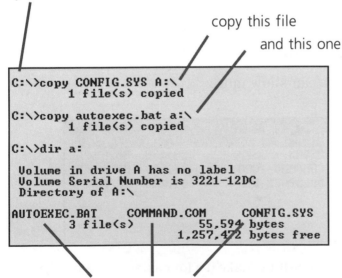

```
C:\>copy CONFIG.SYS A:\
        1 file(s) copied

C:\>copy autoexec.bat a:\
        1 file(s) copied

C:\>dir a:

 Volume in drive A has no label
 Volume Serial Number is 3221-12DC
 Directory of A:\

AUTOEXEC.BAT    COMMAND.COM    CONFIG.SYS
        3 file(s)         55,594 bytes
                       1,257,472 bytes free
```

the disk in drive A: now has copies of these important files

Doublespace

If your computer has been set up to ignore a floppy when it boots, you will need to alter this option if you want to boot from a floppy. Consult the maker's manual concerning the CMOS RAM settings.

The file called DBLSPACE.BIN is present only if your PC uses the Doublespace system.

If your computer has been set up to use Doublespace, you might also use the option of Doublespace on floppy disks. This makes each nominal 1.4 Mbyte disk hold files that would normally take up 2.5 Mbyte or more - the amount of compression depends on the type of file. MS-DOS 6.2 allows you to use ordinary and double-spaced floppies interchangeably - the machine will recognise which type of disk is being used.

The doublespaced disks should be marked, because you cannot format them in the normal way. All the disk actions that you would normally carry out using commands like FORMAT should be avoided on these disks - use the DBLSPACE command instead to bring up the Doublespace menu, and work from there.

A newly created Doublespace floppy contains a small text file (a reminder) and a large (hidden) data file. If your computer is set up to use Doublespace floppies automatically, you will never see these files in a listing.

Take note

If you use Doublespace on floppies, do NOT use it for your backup system disks.

Unformatting a disk

Files are stored as varying magnetic patterns on the disk. When you delete a file, these patterns are not erased, and this is true also of some FORMAT actions.

What is done is to alter the directory information that is held on the disk. These alterations make it seem as if the disk is blank, so that new files can be recorded. If you do not record any new files, the old ones are still there, and can normally be recovered.

The illustration shows the progress of an UNFORMAT command on a floppy disk that was formatted by MS-DOS 6.2 and had originally been formatted using this same version.

```
C:\>unformat A:

Insert disk to rebuild in drive A:
and press ENTER when ready.

Restores the system area of your disk by using the image file created
by the MIRROR command.

       WARNING !!          WARNING !!

This command should be used only to recover from the inadvertent use of
the FORMAT command or the RECOVER command.  Any other use of the UNFORMAT
command may cause you to lose data!  Files modified since the MIRROR image
file was created may be lost.

Searching disk for MIRROR image.

The last time the MIRROR or FORMAT command was used was at 13:09 on 08/03/94.

The MIRROR image file has been validated.

Are you sure you want to update the system area of your drive A (Y/N)?
```

Points

❏ When you format a disk that has been in use, the disk seems blank.

❏ If you originally formatted the disk with a modern version of DOS, MS-DOS 6.0 onwards, you may be able to recover files. If you saw, during formatting, a message about saving UNFORMAT information, then you can recover data using the **UNFORMAT A:** command.

❏ Don't rely on being able to do this - keep proper backups of all files. Only text files can be reliably recovered (though you might be lucky).

The illustration on the opposite page shows what is involved - you place the floppy disk in the drive and type **UNFORMAT A:** (this assumes you are logged to the directory that contains the UNFORMAT program). Because the validation message appears, you could answer Y to this last line, and rebuild the files.

This is a last-chance action. Some files may be in pieces, and though you can often put a file of text together you cannot put a program file together.

Not all formatting can be undone. The FORMAT command can take a /U parameter, which means **u**nconditional. This is sometimes referred to as the File-shredding option, because when **FORMAT A: /U** has been used, nothing can be recovered using UNFORMAT.

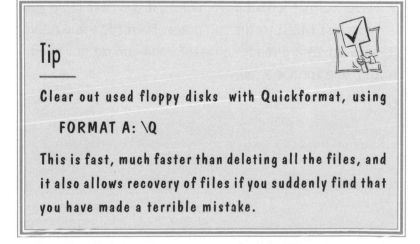

Tip

Clear out used floppy disks with Quickformat, using

   FORMAT A: \Q

This is fast, much faster than deleting all the files, and it also allows recovery of files if you suddenly find that you have made a terrible mistake.

Summary

- ❏ Formatting is needed on a new blank floppy to mark it out for use by a PC machine.

- ❏ If you try to use an unformatted floppy you will get an error message.

- ❏ Formatting takes time, so format a bunch of disks while you are about it.

- ❏ You can use the **/S** parameter to make a System floppy. This holds the MS-DOS system and hidden files, and can be used to boot the computer.

- ❏ You should make several System floppies in case of problems with the hard disk, or in the event of picking up a virus. Using a floppy which was made before any problems arose ensures a clean boot, allowing you to work with your PC until the problems can be resolved.

- ❏ When a format is used on a disk that has files stored on it these files no longer appear in a DIR listing, and the disk can be filled with new files. You can recover the old files before saving any new ones if you use the UNFORMAT command.

- ❏ Never format a hard drive, unless it is a new drive you have just fitted to the computer. Even so, some new hard drives are ready-formatted and you do not need to use a format at all.

NEVER !

format your hard drive. A hard drive is formatted when it is new and before it is put to use, but never again. It can hold thousands of files, and even if recovery is possible for some of them, it won't be possible for all.

DON'T DO IT. NOT EVER. NEVER. When you do, you'll really be glad you had backups of everything.

Remember that no recovery actions are ever possible on a disk that has been formatted and then filled with files.

6 Help!

Selective HELP

The manual for DOS is large, and you cannot always find exactly what you want. There is a HELP system built into modern MS-DOS versions, and though the manual is the ultimate reference for the older versions of MS-DOS, the Help on screen can be very useful.

You can obtain Help in the form of an indexed list, or on specific topics. The indexed list is obtained when you type HELP as a command.

This is shown below. The display gives you some brief instructions about how to see more details of the Help topics by moving the cursor to the item you want and pressing the **[Enter]** key.

Each Help item can consist of several page, with an explanation of the command, list of parameters and their effects, and examples. The Help pages now contain more than the manual, and the manual will often refer you to the Help pages for details.

Basic steps

1 Change to the MS-DOS directory, unless you have a PATH command in force.

2 Type **HELP** [Enter]

3 Use the cursor keys, or the mouse, to move onto the item you want help on.

4 Press **[Enter]** again, or click the mouse.

5 You will see the first Help page on that topic. Use **[Alt]-[N]** for the next page, or **[Alt]-[B]** to move back a page.

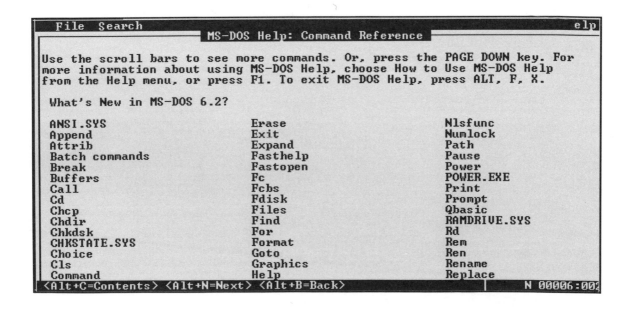

```
  File   Search                                                      elp
                      MS-DOS Help: Command Reference
 Use the scroll bars to see more commands. Or, press the PAGE DOWN key. For
 more information about using MS-DOS Help, choose How to Use MS-DOS Help
 from the Help menu, or press F1. To exit MS-DOS Help, press ALT, F, X.

   What's New in MS-DOS 6.2?

   ANSI.SYS                Erase                 Nlsfunc
   Append                  Exit                  Numlock
   Attrib                  Expand                Path
   Batch commands          Fasthelp              Pause
   Break                   Fastopen              Power
   Buffers                 Fc                    POWER.EXE
   Call                    Fcbs                  Print
   Cd                      Fdisk                 Prompt
   Chcp                    Files                 Qbasic
   Chdir                   Find                  RAMDRIVE.SYS
   Chkdsk                  For                   Rd
   CHKSTATE.SYS            Format                Rem
   Choice                  Goto                  Ren
   Cls                     Graphics              Rename
   Command                 Help                  Replace
 <Alt+C=Contents> <Alt+N=Next> <Alt+B=Back>              N 00006:002
```

If you want help with a particular command, type the command name, followed by a space and /?

This is the display obtained when you type DIR /?

```
Displays a list of files and subdirectories in a directory.

DIR [drive:][path][filename] [/P] [/W] [/A[[:]attribs]] [/O[[:]sortord]]
    [/S] [/B] [/L] [/C[H]]

  [drive:][path][filename]  Specifies drive, directory, and/or files to list.
  /P          Pauses after each screenful of information.
  /W          Uses wide list format.
  /A          Displays files with specified attributes.
  attribs   D  Directories     R  Read-only files        H  Hidden files
            S  System files    A  Files ready to archive  -  Prefix meaning "not
  /O          List by files in sorted order.
  sortord   N  By name (alphabetic)      S  By size (smallest first)
            E  By extension (alphabetic) D  By date & time (earliest first)
            G  Group directories first   -  Prefix to reverse order
            C  By compression ratio (smallest first)
  /S          Displays files in specified directory and all subdirectories.
  /B          Uses bare format (no heading information or summary).
  /L          Uses lowercase.
  /C[H]       Displays file compression ratio; /CH uses host allocation unit size.

Switches may be preset in the DIRCMD environment variable.  Override
preset switches by prefixing any switch with - (hyphen)--for example, /-W.
```

The information is just a summary, to be used as a reminder, not for learning how to use the command.

Help can also be obtained by typing **DOSHELP**. This produces a different list which is even briefer - use it as a reminder of what commands are available.

The DOSHELP display, when the command word is typed with no parameters.

```
C:\>doshelp

For more information on a specific command, type DOSHELP command-name.
APPEND    Allows programs to open data files in specified directories as
          they were in the current directory.
ATTRIB    Displays or changes file attributes.
BREAK     Sets or clears extended CTRL+C checking.
CD        Displays the name of or changes the current directory.
CHCP      Displays or sets the active code page number.
CHDIR     Displays the name of or changes the current directory.
CHKDSK    Checks a disk and displays a status report.
CLS       Clears the screen.
COMMAND   Starts a new instance of the MS-DOS command interpreter.
COMP      Compares the contents of two files or sets of files.
COPY      Copies one or more files to another location.
CTTY      Changes the terminal device used to control your system.
DATE      Displays or sets the date.
DBLSPACE  Sets up or configures DoubleSpace compressed drives.
DEBUG     Starts Debug, a program testing and editing tool.
DEFRAG    Reorganizes the files on a disk to optimize the disk.
DEL       Deletes one or more files.
DELOLDOS  Deletes the OLD_DOS.1 directory and the files it contains.
DELTREE   Deletes a directory and all the files and subdirectories in it.
DIR       Displays a list of files and subdirectories in a directory.
---More---
```

Summary

❑ You can get Help on any DOS command, even when you have just typed the command.

❑ The manuals for modern versions of DOS rely more on these Help pages, and will often refer you to them.

❑ For the most comprehensive Help, type **HELP** as a command. This produces an index of commands, with several pages used for each.

❑ If you have typed a command word, follow it with **/?** to get brief Help notes on that command.

❑ You can get a list of commands, with brief explanations, by using **DOSHELP**.

❑ Using **DOSHELP** with a command name will also produce a brief reminder, the same as that produced by using **/?**.

Tip

Use **/?** for a reminder when you are typing a command, and **HELP** for more detailed information.

7 Copying files

Wildcards

Suppose you have a directory that contains a set of graphics files. Some have the PCX extension, some use GIF, some use TIF, others use BMP. How do you make a list of all the files with the PCX extension?

The simple answer is - use a wildcard, meaning a character that stands in for any set of characters. The character that MS-DOS uses for this purpose is the asterisk *. We have seen this used in a DIR command earlier.

The listing below shows the result of using DIR *.PCX on this sort of mixture of files. The listing shows only the files with the PCX extension letters.

Since the PCX part in the example is typed, it can't be varied, but the * part means any set of characters, so it can mean BEAGGRL, FIG4_13, FIG9_19 and so on.

The result is to list all the PCX files and none of the others. We could have used DIR *.GIF to list all the GIF files, or DIR *.BMP to list all the BMP files.

We could also use DIR FIG4_*.PCX to list files such as FIG4_11. PCX, FIG4_13.PCX and so on, excluding any files that did not start with FIG4_ and end in PCX.

With wildcards you can

❑ obtain a display of selected files in a directory that might contain several hundred.

❑ select groups of files for deleting, copying, or moving.

❑ rename groups of files, as long as they all have some part of their existing name in common.

❑ use this wildcard action with DIR even without typing the asterisk. For example, you could type:

DIR .PCX

and get the same listing as this one.

```
C:\TEMP>dir *.pcx

 Volume in drive C is HARDDISK
 Volume Serial Number is 1401-311C
 Directory of C:\TEMP

BEAGGRL.PCX      BEAGLE.PCX       BEAGPSP.PCX      FIG4_11.PCX      FIG4_12.PCX
FIG4_13.PCX      FIG4_15.PCX      FIG4_16.PCX      FIG4_17.PCX      FIG4_18.PCX
FIG4_19.PCX      FIG8_1.PCX       FIG8_2.PCX       FIG8_3.PCX       FIG8_4.PCX
FIG8_5.PCX       FIG9_19.PCX
        17 file(s)         501,348 bytes
                        60,858,368 bytes free
```

```
C:\PCXFILES\PCPKT>dir fig2_?.pcx

 Volume in drive C is HARDDISK
 Volume Serial Number is 1401-311C
 Directory of C:\PCXFILES\PCPKT

FIG2_2.PCX        FIG2_4.PCX        FIG2_6.PCX        FIG2_7.PCX        FIG2_8.PCX
       5 file(s)              84,705 bytes
                          60,841,984 bytes free
```

- [ ] There is another wildcard, the question mark (?), which stands for any single character.

- [ ] It can be used to select a single-figure range, as shown above.

This listing has been obtained by DIR FIG2_?.PCX. It lists the items where the underscore is followed by a single figure, so it excludes items like FIG2_10.PCX.

Watch it

Some uses of the asterisk wildcard can be dangerous to your files. For example, *.* means all files, and if you delete using this you will be asked to confirm - do you really want to delete all the files in this directory?

delete them all

```
C:\PCXFILES>del *.*
All files in directory will be deleted!
Are you sure (Y/N)?
```

your chance to think again

There are several commands that cannot accept a wildcard as part of a filename. When you try to use these with a wildcard you will get an error message.

```
C:\>type *.txt
Invalid filename or file not found

C:\>ren *.* *.txt
Duplicate file name or file not found
```

Tip

Learn how to use wildcards as they can save a lot of effort.

Backing up to a Floppy

Backing up files is one of the most important computing actions. Unless you can replace your hard drive at suitable intervals, assuming you knew what these were, it will some day refuse to boot. You might be able to get access to it after using a System floppy, but you might not. Where, then, are all these files you created over the last few years?

The answer, if you are sensible, is that you have backup copies on floppy disks. You should have the original distribution disks for all your programs, you have several System floppies for MS-DOS, and you should also use floppies to save spare copies of all your precious data.

1 Log on to the directory whose files you want to copy.

2 Make sure that you have a formatted floppy in the A: drive - with enough space on it for the files you are going to copy.

3 Use the **COPY** command in the form:

   COPY source dest

   For example:

   COPY *.* A:

   to copy all the files in the directory to the floppy.

4 You will see each filename listed as it is copied.

source directory   copy to floppy

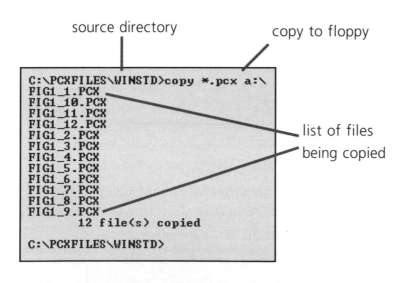

```
C:\PCXFILES\WINSTD>copy *.pcx a:\
FIG1_1.PCX
FIG1_10.PCX
FIG1_11.PCX
FIG1_12.PCX
FIG1_2.PCX
FIG1_3.PCX
FIG1_4.PCX
FIG1_5.PCX
FIG1_6.PCX
FIG1_7.PCX
FIG1_8.PCX
FIG1_9.PCX
        12 file(s) copied

C:\PCXFILES\WINSTD>
```

list of files
being copied

now use DIR A: to check the list

copy | WHAT TO COPY | DESTINATION

Simple and safe

5 After copying, check that the files are safely there by using

DIR A:

(A: in this example) Never assume that all is well until you see this listing.

The key to making useful backups is the use of the COPY command in its simplest form, as illustrated. COPY has to be followed by two arguments. One is the source - what file is to be copied - you can use a wildcard to indicate a set of files. The other is the destination, a drive or a directory.

Backing up your data is not a luxury; it is an essential. Only you know what data files you have and what they contain, and if you lose them no-one can replace them for you. The program files that you have bought will still be on their floppy disks, safely tucked away, and you should keep copies of your data files also.

MS-DOS contains a rather complicated form of BACKUP command which allows you to back up selected parts of your hard disk to floppies.

You need a lot of floppies if you want to back up the whole hard disk, 80 or more floppies is not uncommon. If you need to back up all or nearly all of the contents of a hard disk, use a tape streamer or an optical disk which can hold large amounts of data, rather than floppies.

Take note

If you are tempted by backing up systems that allow you to save huge amounts of data, ask for a demonstration. Some will only return data to the disk they were saved from, which isn't very useful if that disk has just disintegrated. Terrible disappointments have awaited those who never tried out their backup system until it was needed.

Painless backup

Notes

Backing up to floppies is not always quite so straightforward. Suppose, for example that you have laboured over a hot computer all day to create data files that amount to some 2.4 Mbyte. You won't get this lot on to a single floppy, and they might not even fit exactly on to two.

MS-DOS is not very co-operative about copying large numbers of files. Ideally, you could start such a copy and you would be told when to change disks. Windows does that, but not MS-DOS.

DOSSHELL is much better for making backups of groups of files. It still won't tell you to change disks, but it does allow you to select groups of files to copy, and shows the space they need. You can select files until you have enough to fill a disk.

❏ It's a lot easier just to back up your data as you create it, using **COPY**.

❏ This avoids the problem of struggling a huge set of files later. You have to add up the file sizes to find how many will fit on one disk. Having copied these, you do another group and so on. The trouble is, you can't use wildcards for these groups.

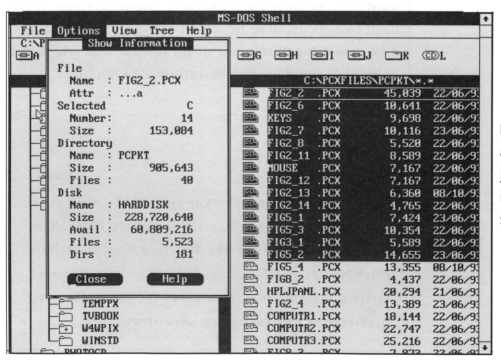

DOSSHELL does a rather better job of it, as this illustration shows.

Floppy to Floppy

- If you make a backup each time you save a data file the process is almost painless. Many programs have a SAVE AS command for this purpose.

- There is an XCOPY command which will save only the files that have been changed since the last time you saved files. An example of its use will be illustrated later.

- If you have more than one hard disk, you might be tempted to keep backups on one of them. *Don't do it.*

You can also copy files from one floppy disk to another. Most modern computers have only one floppy drive, and the command for copying files from a floppy disk to another floppy disk is not obvious. For example:

COPY A:*.PCX   B:

will copy all the files with the extension letters of PCX from a disk in the floppy drive to another disk in the drive. The puzzling thing about this is the use of **B:**.

If you have two floppy drives, they will be referred to as A: and B:. If you have only one drive, it also can be referred to as A: or B:. When you use the COPY command illustrated above, you will be asked to insert the source disk in the A: drive. After some time, you will be asked to insert the disk for B:, and this is your destination disk.

On older versions of MS-DOS you might need to swap the disks more than once - make sure you label them clearly before you start.

Copying between directories

The other important copy actions are from one directory to another, and from a floppy to a hard disk directory. Copying from one directory to another on the hard drive is a very fast operation.

When you copy from one directory to another each directory path must be provided. There are some short cuts, but these are best avoided until you have more experience.

One posible shortcut is that the current directory will be used as the destination if you do not specify a destination in the COPY command. This is illustrated below, and it also shows how the files are listed as they are copied, so that you do not need to use DIR to see the files.

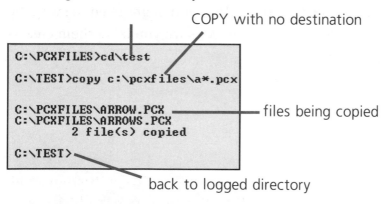

log onto this directory

COPY with no destination

```
C:\PCXFILES>cd\test
C:\TEST>copy c:\pcxfiles\a*.pcx

C:\PCXFILES\ARROW.PCX
C:\PCXFILES\ARROWS.PCX
        2 file(s) copied
C:\TEST>
```

files being copied

back to logged directory

The copy action for copying files from a floppy to a hard disk directory is of just the same form:

For example:

    COPY A:*.* C:\TEXT

will copy all the files from the floppy in the A: drive into a directory called TEXT on the hard drive.

Rules

1 You cannot copy a file or a set of files to the same directory or to the same floppy (unless you are copying to a sub-directory on the floppy). In other words, you cannot copy a file to itself.

2 You can use a wildcard to represent the source files, or the destination files, but not the destination directory.

- You can rename files as you copy them, see later.

- You can alter the date and time information on files as you copy them, see later.

- You can use COPY to print files, see later.

Take note

COPY creates another file with the same name. If you want to move a file from one place to another, there is a MOVE command in modern versions of DOS. With older DOS versions, use a COPY followed by a DEL to delete the files.

For example, if you are logged to C:\TXTFILE and use :

> COPY C:\EXAMPLE\TEXT*.TXT

this will copy all files with the TXT extension to the current directory called C:\TEXTFILE.

This use of COPY with no destination directory has to be used carefully - you can easily forget what directory you are logged to, though modern versions of DOS show the logged directory as part of the prompt.

Copying and Installing Programs

A few programs that are distributed on floppy disks require you to create a directory on the hard drive and copy files from a floppy into that directory. Most modern programs contain SETUP or INSTALL utilities. You put the first of a set of floppies into the drive, type SETUP (or INSTALL) and the program does all the rest. Very often the files are stored in compressed form, and just copying them would not be enough.

Move

The MOVE command can be used on MS-DOS 6.0 onwards. The action is shown here - note that the source file is deleted only when the copy has been verified.

MOVE is used like COPY

each move is verified

```
A:\>move *.pcx c:\temp

a:\arrow.pcx => c:\temp\arrow.pcx [ok]
a:\arrows.pcx => c:\temp\arrows.pcx [ok]
a:\newrow.pcx => c:\temp\newrow.pcx [ok]
```

Verifying a copy

You can modify the COPY command with the parameter /
V, as illustrated below. V means verify, and it makes the
machine check that each file has been copied.

It does not, however, check that the copy is *identical* –
nor is there a message to tell you that the files are
verified. Using the /V addition also makes the COPY
command run rather slower.

DIR or DIR /W (to get the detailed listing) will show you if
the copy has the same number of bytes as the original.
But if you want to check that a file copy is *exactly* the
same as the original, there is a special command for that
purpose, **FC**.

Take note

If your dircmd has been
set so that **DIR** nor-
mally produces a wide
(names only) listing you
will have to use:

DIR /-W

to get a detailed list. If
dircmd has not been set,
a simple **DIR** produces
the detailed list.

request verification

... but no message that the
files are verified

check the copying

```
C:\TEST>copy *.pcx a: /V
ARROW.PCX
ARROWS.PCX
        2 file(s) copied


C:\TEST>dir a:

 Volume in drive A has no label
 Volume Serial Number is 3221-12DC
 Directory of A:\

ARROW.PCX         ARROWS.PCX
        2 file(s)              10,360 bytes
                          1,303,040 bytes free

C:\TEST>
```

Comparing files

If you want real file verification you need to use the FC command.

In this example, FC indicates that the copy is identical.

comparison command

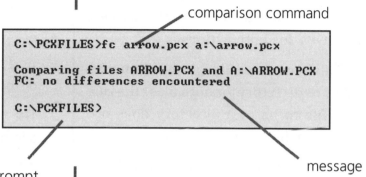

```
C:\PCXFILES>fc arrow.pcx a:\arrow.pcx

Comparing files ARROW.PCX and A:\ARROW.PCX
FC: no differences encountered

C:\PCXFILES>
```

back to prompt

message

In the next example, the FC test shows two differences. FC is more often used to check for deliberate changes made by editing than for file corruption after copying.

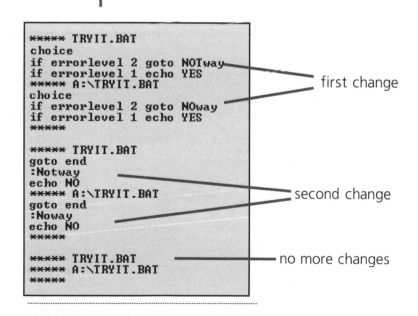

```
***** TRYIT.BAT
choice
if errorlevel 2 goto NOTway
if errorlevel 1 echo YES
***** A:\TRYIT.BAT
choice
if errorlevel 2 goto NOway
if errorlevel 1 echo YES
*****

***** TRYIT.BAT
goto end
:Notway
echo NO
***** A:\TRYIT.BAT
goto end
:Noway
echo NO
*****

***** TRYIT.BAT
***** A:\TRYIT.BAT
*****
```

first change

second change

no more changes

Renaming with COPY

Rename

COPY is a very versatile command. It can rename a file that is being copied, and it can attach a file to the end of another. In both cases, the original files are left intact.

These actions can also be carried out by **REN** and by text editor programs, but if you need the COPY action as well, it saves time to use COPY for both actions.

When you COPY and also rename a file in one action, you can use the same drive or directory for both files - the rule about not copying a file to its own directory does not apply when the name is being changed.

This example shows copying with rename and with appending.

1 For the source file, type the full path (unless you are logged to the correct directory) and full filename.

2 For the destination, type the full path and a different filename.

3 The file will be copied and renamed when you press the **[Enter]** key.

copy and rename

check that files are there

copy and append

```
A:\>copy arrow.pcx narrow.old
        1 file(s) copied

A:\>dir

 Volume in drive A has no label
 Volume Serial Number is 3221-12DC
 Directory of A:\

ARROW.PCX        ARROWS.PCX        NARROW.OLD        TRYIT.BAT
        4 file(s)              11,415 bytes
                           1,301,504 bytes free


A:\>copy arrow.pcx+narrow.old+arrows.pcx newrow.pcx
ARROW.PCX
NARROW.OLD
ARROWS.PCX
        1 file(s) copied

A:\>dir

 Volume in drive A has no label
 Volume Serial Number is 3221-12DC
 Directory of A:\

ARROW.PCX        ARROWS.PCX        NARROW.OLD        NEWROW.PCX        TRYIT.BAT
        5 file(s)              10,800 bytes
                           1,301,504 bytes free
```

Demonstration only – only text files can be appended succesfully.

74

Appending with COPY

Append

1 Following COPY, type the names (with path if needed) of the files to be attached, using a + sign between them, such as:

   COPY FILEA+FILEB

2 Follow this with the destination filename (with path if needed) and press **[Enter]**.

3 The files, **FILEA** and **FILEB** in this example, will be combined, using the name of the destination file.

❑ When files are copied, the copy bears the same time and date information as the original.

❑ You can alter this by adding the symbols **+,,** to the source filename (but not if you are using a wildcard).

You can use COPY to attach a file to the end of another. This is called *appending*. Only simple text files can be appended successfully. Appended files of any other type can rarely be used by the program that created them. Joining PCX files will NOT make a joined image.

When you append files, attaching one to another, you cannot make the destination have the same name as one of the files. You will be reminded if you do this.

You can append files using a wildcard and no + sign. For example:

   COPY FIL?.TXT ALLTX

will add **FIL1.TXT, FIL2.TXT** etc. to a file called **ALLTX**.

use narrow directory
to get date and time

note date
and time

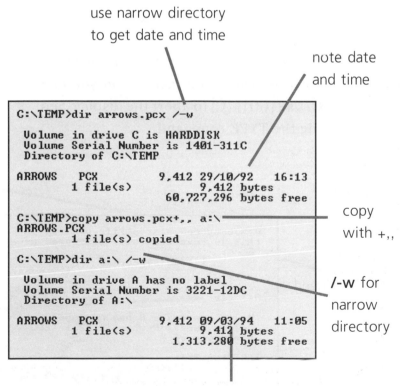

```
C:\TEMP>dir arrows.pcx /-w

 Volume in drive C is HARDDISK
 Volume Serial Number is 1401-311C
 Directory of C:\TEMP

ARROWS     PCX         9,412 29/10/92   16:13
           1 file(s)           9,412 bytes
                        60,727,296 bytes free
C:\TEMP>copy arrows.pcx+,, a:\
ARROWS.PCX
           1 file(s) copied

C:\TEMP>dir a:\ /-w

 Volume in drive A has no label
 Volume Serial Number is 3221-12DC
 Directory of A:\

ARROWS     PCX         9,412 09/03/94   11:05
           1 file(s)           9,412 bytes
                         1,313,280 bytes free
```

copy
with +,,

/-w for
narrow
directory

new date and time appears on this copy

COPYing to devices

The COPY command has yet another use in copying file to devices. Device in this sense means something that is not a file, but which can be referred to with a name like a file.

The main names that can be used in this way are CON, PRN (or LPT1) and NUL. You can also use COM1 or AUX, but these refer to the serial port, and most PC owners do not need to control the serial port with DOS commands.

The CON name is an abbreviation of CONSOLE. When you use CON as the source of a file, the keyboard will be used. When you use CON as the destination of a file, the monitor screen will be used.

Using **COPY CON filename**, as illustrated, is a useful way of creating short text files. **COPY file CON** is useful for viewing short text files, but not long files because the screen will scroll faster than you can read the text. Use [Ctrl]-[C] to abort the display. See later for using the TYPE command.

❑ **To create a text file**

1 Type :

   COPY CON filename

   using a full path for your filename as required.

2 Type the text that you want to put into the file. The **[Enter]** key will create a new line of text.

3 When you want to stop typing and record the file, press the **[Ctrl]-[Z]** keys together. This shows as **^Z** on the screen.

Copy from CON

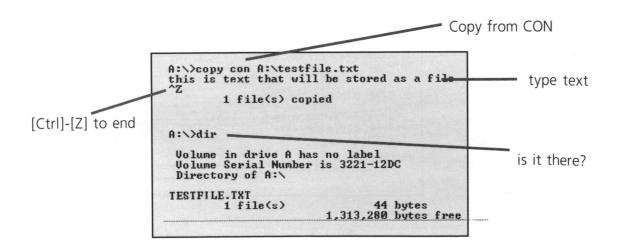

type text

[Ctrl]-[Z] to end

is it there?

```
A:\>copy con A:\testfile.txt
this is text that will be stored as a file
^Z
        1 file(s) copied

A:\>dir

 Volume in drive A has no label
 Volume Serial Number is 3221-12DC
 Directory of A:\

TESTFILE.TXT
        1 file(s)                      44 bytes
                          1,313,280 bytes free
```

Basic steps

To view a text file

1 Locate the file and log to its directory.

2 Type:

COPY filename CON

and press **[Enter]**

You will see the text appear on the screen.

3 If there is more text than will fit in the screen, it will scroll - the lines at the top will vanish as new lines are added at the bottom.

Printing with COPY

The printer can be referred to as **PRN** or **LPT1**. For example, you can print a text file called MYTX.TXT using the command:

COPY MYTX.TXT PRN

- remember the printer must be connected and on line.

You can also copy from CON to PRN to make the keyboard print directly. This is best done with a dot-matrix or bubblejet printer, because you can better control where the printing appears on the paper.

connects the keyboard to the printer

the ^N is not printed

```
C:\>copy con prn

This is text to be printed^N
The Ctrl-N keys force a new line on the printer-^N
but you need to use the ENTER key to get a new line^N
on the screen.^N
Press Ctrl+Z to start printing, Ctrl+C to abort

^Z
```

end of action - printer disconnected

You may need to use the FORM FEED button on a laser printer to start the printing.

COPY to CON

```
A:\>copy testfile.txt con
this is text that will be stored as a file
        1 file(s) copied
```

Summary

❏ The **wildcard** characters are ***** and **?**, and they are used to replace part of a filename that is used as an argument for a command.

❏ You can use these wildcards in a main name or in an extension or both, but not in a path.

❏ Wildcards allow you to apply commands to groups of files, making some actions on groups almost as fast as an action on a single file.

❏ You need to take care about using ***.*** which means any file.

❏ The **COPY** command is one of the most important in MS-DOS, and it can be used in a variety of ways.

❏ The main use is in the form **COPY source destination,** to copy a file to a different drive or directory. In this case, source is the filename (might include path) for the file being copied, and destination is the new drive letter and/or directory path.

❏ You can **rename** a file as it is being copied, by using a different filename for the destination.

❏ You can **append** (join) files using COPY, though this is useful only for text files.

❏ You can **change the date and time** of a file to the current date and time by using COPY in the form **COPY sourcefile+,, destfile**.

❏ You can also use COPY with **devices**, meaning keyboard and screen, printer and serial port.

Take note

If you run **MS-DOS** from **Windows**, do **NOT** use **COPY CON PRN** as you cannot disengage the printer with **[Ctrl]-[C]**. You will have to save any open files, and use **Ctrl-Alt-Del** to escape.

8 Managing files

Renaming a file

Renaming a file is needed more often than you might think. It does not make a new copy of a file.

The most common reason is that you have been using a program that generates data files, such as a word-processor, and you have just named and saved a file. You then realise that you have mis-spelled the name or that you would prefer to use another name.

Another reason might be that you have a program that reads text files, for example, but only if their extension letters are TXT. Your text files use DOC, or perhaps you did not use any extension letters. Once again, you need to rename these files.

1 Locate the file that you want to rename - you might want to log on to its directory and check that it is present with DIR.

2 Type the rename command in the form:

   REN old new

where **old** is the name you want to change and **new** is the desired name.

3 Press **[Enter]**, and check when the action is completed that the renaming has been done.

rename this file

that's it

```
A:\>ren readme.txt oldinfo.doc

A:\>
A:\>dir

 Volume in drive A has no label
 Volume Serial Number is 3221-12DC
 Directory of A:\

ADDTHEM.TXT      BOOTLOG.TXT      LICENSE.TXT      NEWFILE.TXT      OLDINFO.TXT
PACKAGE.TXT      READWHOP.TXT     SETUP.TXT        TESTFILE.TXT
         9 file(s)             60,737 bytes
                            1,250,816 bytes free

A:\>ren addthem.txt oldinfo.doc
Duplicate file name or file not found

A:\>
```

you can't use an existing name

With REN you cannot

- ❏ Rename only data files that you have created for yourself. Do not rename those that are part of program suites. For example, the word-processor program Word uses a file called NORMAL.DOT. Any attempt to rename this will cause considerable problems in using Word.

- ❏ rename a file if there is already a file in the same directory that bears the name you want to use. You will get the **Duplicate File Name or File Not Found** error message.

- ❏ place the new named file in a different directory - use the renaming action of COPY for that purpose.

- ❏ rename a directory (but you can with MOVE).

- ❏ rename a disk label (use the LABEL command)

Take note

You get no form of acknowledgement of a rename action. Use a **DIR** to check that the new name exists.

Renaming directories

When the REN command was first put into MS-DOS, directories were not used much, and the possibility of renaming directories was not considered.

Since MS-DOS version 5.0, it has been possible to rename a directory using DOSSHELL, but renaming a directory with DOS has only been possible since Version 6.0

This illustrates renaming a directory by using the MOVE command. It shows also the importance of listing the directories before and after such a change, so that you can see what you have done.

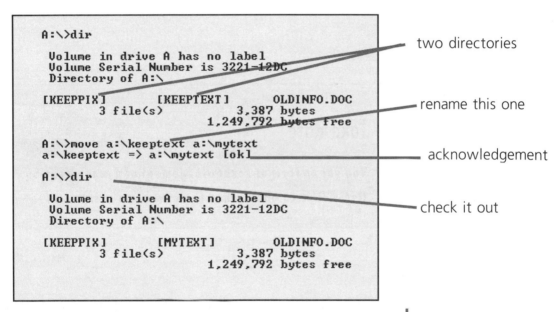

```
A:\>dir

 Volume in drive A has no label
 Volume Serial Number is 3221-12DC
 Directory of A:\

[KEEPPIX]        [KEEPTEXT]       OLDINFO.DOC
        3 file(s)              3,387 bytes
                          1,249,792 bytes free

A:\>move a:\keeptext a:\mytext
a:\keeptext => a:\mytext [ok]

A:\>dir

 Volume in drive A has no label
 Volume Serial Number is 3221-12DC
 Directory of A:\

[KEEPPIX]        [MYTEXT]         OLDINFO.DOC
        3 file(s)              3,387 bytes
                          1,249,792 bytes free
```

two directories

rename this one

acknowledgement

check it out

You cannot alter the position of a directory you rename using MOVE. For example, you cannot do:

    MOVE C:\OLDTEXT   C:\FILES\MYTEXT

which tries to create a directory that is a sub-directory of C:\FILES. The renamed directory must occupy the same place in the tree as it had under its old name.

Using wildcards with REN

This shows wildcards being used with REN, for the common task of changing the extension letters of a set of files, something that can be done very quickly with REN.

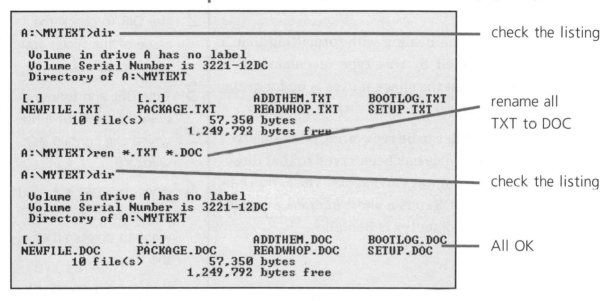

```
A:\MYTEXT>dir
```
— check the listing
```
 Volume in drive A has no label
 Volume Serial Number is 3221-12DC
 Directory of A:\MYTEXT

[.]              [..]            ADDTHEM.TXT     BOOTLOG.TXT
NEWFILE.TXT      PACKAGE.TXT     READWHOP.TXT    SETUP.TXT
        10 file(s)              57,350 bytes
                             1,249,792 bytes free

A:\MYTEXT>ren *.TXT *.DOC
```
— rename all TXT to DOC
```
A:\MYTEXT>dir
```
— check the listing
```
 Volume in drive A has no label
 Volume Serial Number is 3221-12DC
 Directory of A:\MYTEXT

[.]              [..]            ADDTHEM.DOC     BOOTLOG.DOC
NEWFILE.DOC      PACKAGE.DOC     READWHOP.DOC    SETUP.DOC
        10 file(s)              57,350 bytes
                             1,249,792 bytes free
```
— All OK

Impossible renaming

Take note

When you use wildcards with **REN** in this way, the letters that the wildcard represents in the first name are also used in the second name. There are limits to this as the examples show.

REN only works if the renaming is totally unambiguous. The computer can only work on the data that you give it, and a command must have only one possible outcome.

REN C:\CHAP?.TXT CHAP2.TXT

will not work if there is a file called CHAP2.TXT in this directory. If there is no CHAP2.TXT already , one file will be changed to that name, and from then no more.

REN C:\CHAP?.TXT CHAP1?.TXT

also does not work (it cannot change CHAP1.TXT into CHAP11.TXT). As far as the computer is concerned, CHAP1 is the same as CHAP?, so the filename are read no further - the computer treats these as being the same.

Deleting files

The DEL command is an abbreviation of Delete, and you can also use ERASE (but it takes longer to type). It has to be followed by a filename, separated by a space, and you can use wildcards.

We've seen earlier when dealing with formatting that a file is not really deleted by this type of command. It remains on the disk, but the space it uses is up for grabs if another file is saved on the same disk or directory.

This allows "deleted" files to be recovered, or un-deleted, providing that nothing else has been saved to that directory since the DEL action was carried out. The action can be made easier if MS-DOS runs a short unerase program at the time when the computer is booted.

Basic steps

1 Log on to the disk or directory where the files are located.

2 Use **DIR** to check the name of the file(s) you want to delete.

3 Type **DEL** and follow it with the name of a file, which can contain a wildcard.

4 If you use **DEL *.***, you are asked if you really want to delete all of the files.

You are not asked to confirm with a single wildcard, like ***.TXT** or **EXAMPLE.***.

check files first

delete this one

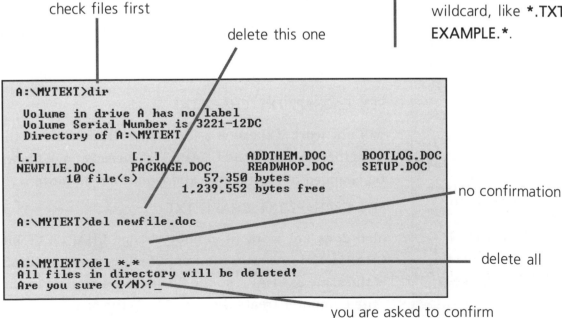

```
A:\MYTEXT>dir

   Volume in drive A has no label
   Volume Serial Number is 3221-12DC
   Directory of A:\MYTEXT

[.]              [..]              ADDTHEM.DOC      BOOTLOG.DOC
NEWFILE.DOC      PACKAGE.DOC       READWHOP.DOC     SETUP.DOC
        10 file(s)            57,350 bytes
                           1,239,552 bytes free


A:\MYTEXT>del newfile.doc


A:\MYTEXT>del *.*
All files in directory will be deleted!
Are you sure (Y/N)?_
```

no confirmation

delete all

you are asked to confirm

Examples

DEL C:\TEXT\FILA.TXT

> will delete FILA.TXT in
> the C:\TEXT directory.

DEL C:\TEXT*.TXT

> will delete all TXT files
> in this directory.

DEL C:\TEXT*.*

> will delete all files of
> any type in this direc-
> tory, and you will be
> asked if you really want
> to do this.

Keeping the root files safe

A few common-sense precautions on the way you use
your hard disk can avoid the calamity of deleting the root
directory. You might never type DEL C:*.*, but you
might quite easily type **DEL *.*** not realising that you
were using the root directory.

Place into the C:\ root directory only the few files that are
essential - these are the hidden/system files, along with
AUTOEXEC.BAT and CONFIG.SYS. If you use Doublespace
then DBLSPACE.BIN will be included. Keep backups of all
these. All other MS-DOS files, including COMMAND.COM,
ca be held in a directory called MSDOS or DOS (if you have
installed any version of DOS from 5.0 onwards, this will
have been done for you automatically.).

Now if you delete the root directory there is not so much
to lose, and it can be recovered if you use the UNDELETE
command immediately. (See over.)

It's better not to delete the root directory, but nobody's
perfect.

Take note

**Never type DEL C:*.*.
It will delete all the
files in the root direc-
tory of the hard disk,
and you will need a lot
of effort to restore
things.**

Undeleting files

Undeleting a deleted file is possible only if nothing else has been saved using the same space - if the file is valuable you have nothing to lose by trying an undelete even if other data has been saved.

You may be lucky - quite often a new file that is saved uses a different part of the disk, leaving your deleted files intact. This, however, applies only if the disk is fairly empty.

The conventional method, illustrated below, requires you to supply the first letter for each filename. This does not need to be the original start letter, as long as a change does not cause a conflict (two files with the same name).

The alternatives to UNDELETE are Tracker and Sentry. These were first used in MS-DOS 5.0.

1 Log on to the directory that held the deleted files.

2 Type

   UNDELETE

   and press [Enter].

3 You will be asked for a file specification. You must use a wildcard - you cannot give the name of the file as it has gone! ***.*** is often the best.

4 If UNDELETE finds a file that you want, give a first letter.

you must use a wildcard

we are not using these systems on this PC

```
undelete
Directory: A:\MYTEXT
File Specifications: *.*

    Delete Sentry control file not found.

    Deletion-tracking file not found.

    MS-DOS directory contains    2 deleted files.
    Of those,    2 files may be recovered.
Using the MS-DOS directory method.

    ?EWFILE  DOC        84  9/03/94 12:08   ...A  Undelete (Y/N)?y
    Please type the first character for ?EWFILE .DOC: N

File successfully undeleted.

    ?DDTHEM  DOC      6436  9/03/94 14:26   ...A  Undelete (Y/N)?y
    Please type the first character for ?DDTHEM .DOC: A

File successfully undeleted.
```

give a first letter

Methods

Both Sentry and Tracker need a command, and this must be carried out before you delete any files.

The best place for these commands is in the AUTOEXEC.BAT file, which runs as soon as MS-DOS is loaded. Don't rely on your memory – automate.

Sentry also needs a line in the AUTOEXEC.BAT file, and its installation is much the same as for Tracker.

Sentry and tracker

Sentry creates a small file on the drive and uses a memory-resident program. It offers high security against loss, but at the cost of using an appreciable amount of disk space. It also has a habit of leaving small but unerasable files on floppy disks.

Tracker does not place any file on the disk, but uses a short memory-resident program. It offers as much security as most users require.

Both Sentry and Tracker make the un-deletion action virtually automatic. They each provide enough information to restore a file without the need to type a first letter.

Delete Tracker is installed by using the command:

UNDELETE /TA-50

This will enable tracking for the hard drive, and for up to 50 files on a floppy. When you subsequently delete files and use UNDELETE, Sentry will be tried, then Tracker, giving the screen display shown below:

```
    Deletion-tracking file contains    1 deleted files.
    Of those,    1 files have all clusters available,
                 0 files have some clusters available,
                 0 files have no clusters available.

    MS-DOS directory contains   27 deleted files.
    Of those,   25 files may be recovered.

Using the Deletion-tracking method.

    OLDINFO  DOC      3387  3/06/92 23:09   ...A  Deleted:  9/03/94 16:40
All of the clusters for this file are available. Undelete (Y/N)?y

File successfully undeleted.
```

The Tracker program has maintained a record of the first letter of the filename and other details for the deleted files, and it allows restoration with little fuss or bother.

Deleting Directories

The older method for deleting directories uses the RD or RMDIR (Remove Directory) command, but this requires a bit of effort on your part before you can use it.

You must make sure that the directory you are going to delete contains no files and no sub-directories of its own (which might also have files and sub-directories).

To delete a sub-directory, you must first log on to another directory - the easiest is the parent directory.

In the example below, the directory MYTEXT is a sub-directory of the root directory A:\ on a floppy disk.

Tip

Always have a printout of your TREE layout at hand before you start to delete any directories.

1 Get a listing for the directory, to find if there are any files or sub-directories.

2 If there are sub-directories, get listings for them, and delete their files and sub-directories first, as described below.

3 Delete the all files in the directory, using

   DEL *.*

4 Log on one stage nearer the root, with

   CD ..

5 Use RD, giving the name of the directory. For example:

   RD C:\TEMPDIR

check what's there

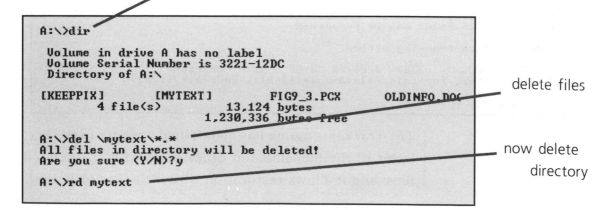

```
A:\>dir

 Volume in drive A has no label
 Volume Serial Number is 3221-12DC
 Directory of A:\

[KEEPPIX]        [MYTEXT]          FIG9_3.PCX      OLDINFO.DOC
        4 file(s)          13,124 bytes
                        1,230,336 bytes free

A:\>del \mytext\*.*
All files in directory will be deleted!
Are you sure (Y/N)?y

A:\>rd mytext
```

delete files

now delete directory

RD rules

1 The directory must not contain any files.

2 The directory must not have any sub-directories.

3 The command cannot be used while you are logged on to the directory you want to delete.

4 You cannot delete the root directory of any disk.

5 You cannot delete a directory that contains hidden or system files.

Hidden files?

If you think you have cleared a directory completely (and the DIR command shows no files in that directory) but you get an error message about not being able to delete because the directory is not empty, the cause is usually hidden files. Before you go to the effort of listing these files and deleting them, ask yourself why they are there - they are probably required by a program, and it might not be a program that you have deleted.

Take note

You cannot use the **UNDELETE** command to restore a deleted directory. If you delete a directory unintentionally, you will have to re-create it, see later.

The effort that you need, of deleting files and sub-directories, should help to avoid deleting a directory in error.

Using DELTREE

Using RD to remove a directory can be slow, and there are faster ways. One of these is DELTREE, but you need some confidence in your backup system to use this one.

The DELTREE command was introduced with MS-DOS 6.0, and it can remove directories along with their sub-directories and files, instead of having to remove them separately. You can use DELTREE followed by more than one argument (separating the arguments by spaces).

For example a line such as:

DELTREE C:\TEMPFILE   C:\DOS\OLDBITS

will remove the two named directories, all the files they contain, and any sub-directories they contain. DELTREE can be used with a wildcard - but unless you have immense confidence you should never try it.

The illustration shows this command in use to remove a directory on a floppy disk:

Basic steps

1 Start work from the parent directory of the one you want to delete, or the root, whichever is more convenient.

2 Type **DELTREE**, then a space.

3 Follow this with the name (with path) for the first directory you want to delete.

4 You can add other directories (each with path), but not the one you are currently using.

delete this directory

```
A:\>dir

  Volume in drive A has no label
  Volume Serial Number is 3221-12DC
  Directory of A:\

[KEEPPIX]        FIG9_3.PCX        OLDINFO.DOC
      3 file(s)            13,124 bytes
                       1,290,240 bytes free

A:\>deltree keeppix
Delete directory "keeppix" and all its subdirectories? [yn]
Deleting keeppix...
```

request for confirmation

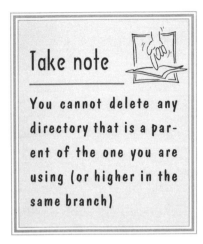
The use of DOSSHELL is much simpler and safer than any other methods using MS-DOS directly. It allows you to clear out files and delete an empty directory quickly, though not as quickly as DELTREE.

DOSSHELL is intended to be used along with a mouse, and though it can be used from the keyboard you lose many of its advantages when you work in that way.

You can delete all the files in a directory without using the mouse - simply log on to the directory files list and choose the **Select All item** from the **Files** menu. This will mark the files, and you can then use the **[Delete]** key to delete the files and then the directory.

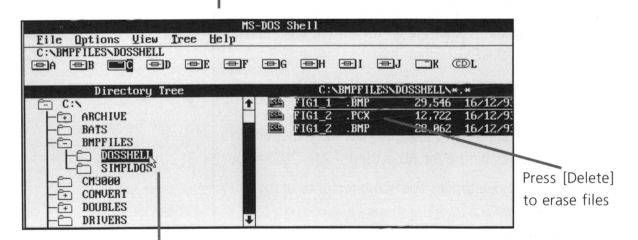

Press [Delete] to erase files

and again to delete directory

Using DOSSHELL, you can see the file names you are deleting, and the empty directory is deleted simply by placing the cursor over the name of the directory and clicking the mouse button. Normally, you will find that the cursor is on the name of the empty directory in any case, so your actions, after marking all the files, consist simply of pressing the **[Delete]** key twice.

Summary

- ❑ A file can be renamed using **REN**, followed by the names of the old file and the new file in that order.

- ❑ Renaming does not create a new copy - the old file simply has a new name

- ❑ You cannot rename a file if the same name already exists in the same directory.

- ❑ Wildcards can be used in a **REN** command, but only to a limited extent.

- ❑ To delete a file, use **DEL** followed by a file name or wildcard expression.

- ❑ A wildcard can be used so as to delete a group of files, such as files that share the same extension.

- ❑ If you use **DEL *.*** to delete all the files in a directory, you will be asked to confirm this.

- ❑ Deleted files can be recovered by **UNDELETE**. Undeletion is easier if you install Tracker.

- ❑ To delete a directory, it must be cleared of files and sub-directories before the **RD** is used.

- ❑ **DELTREE** will delete files and sub-directories along with the directory.

- ❑ **DOSSHELL** offers a simple and safe way of deleting a directory.

- ❑ A deleted directory cannot be undeleted.

9 Text files

What is a text file?

A text file has a special status in MS-DOS, because there are more commands that can be used relating to text files than to other files.

The reasons are mainly historical. In the early days of DOS there were only program files and text files. Programs were written as lines of instructions which were saved as text files, and these text files were converted into program files.

Dealing with text files was therefore a very important part of DOS at a time when DOS was used mainly by program writers because each program started as a text file - and it still does.

The illustration below shows a composite view of a text file and a program file printed out. It was obtained with DOSSHELL, using the [F9] key to show the characters and codes of a file on screen.

A text file..

❑ consists of characters that have standard ASCII codes of 32 to 127, see opposite.

❑ is marked at the end with the code number that is put in by pressing [Ctrl]-[Z]. This is ASCII code number 31.

❑ can be displayed on the screen without any strange characters appearing, and it can be printed.

❑ can be appended to another, using COPY, to create a larger file.

```
@echo off
if %1==% goto noparm
if %2==% goto noparm
cd %1
md %2
a:
echo Please wait...copying files.
copy a:*.* %1\%2 > nul
echo All done - files in %1\%2
goto endit
:noparm
echo Need to supply root directory and name
echo for new directory.
:endit
c:\
```

Text file (a batch file)   Program file

ASCII codes

- can be created with the resources of MS-DOS, see later.

- can be viewed or printed with the TYPE and PRINT commands, see later in this Section.

As someone once said of the elephant, you might not be able to define it, but you know it when you see it.

ASCII codes are named after the initial letters of American Standards Committee for Information Interchange, who devised the codes. You do not need to know what number is used for each character.

The numbers 32 to 127 are used as codes for all the letters of the alphabet, uppercase and lowercase, the numerals 0 to 9, and a set of punctuation marks and assorted signs like the dollar, ampersand and asterisk. There is no ASCII code for a pound sterling.

The numbers 0 to 31, and 128 to 255 are used for other purposes, some for characters that are not in the ASCII set. The code 31 (which can be obtained by using the keys **[Ctrl]-[Z]** is used in all text files to mean *End of Text*.

When you use the COPY command on a text file, it will copy everything up to the code 31 entry. When you append files using COPY, the ASCII 31 codes are deleted except for the last one.

Looking at files

The text file contains only recognisable characters and is usually arranged into lines. The program file contains mainly unrecognisable characters and has no form of line arrangement. This makes it easy to recognise the difference when you see a file displayed on the screen.

A program file may contain some text - the identification names used by a program, and any error messages have to be stored as part of it. When you see text, mixed with unrecognisable characters, this is likely to be a program.

The illustration at the foot of the page shows pieces of text that are embedded inside a program file. You can still tell that this is not a text file, however.

The strange-looking characters in a program arise because programs use codes 0 to 255 - they are not restricted to the ASCII range of 32 to 127.

Files from a word-processor often contain similar characters, usually grouped at the start or the end of the file. These are the codes for such items as page size, margins, tabs, fonts and so on. A simple text editor does not use these codes, only the ASCII range.

1 Find your text file. Extension like TXT or DOC are a clue, as also is a main name such as README. Avoid files with extensions such as COM, EXE, DLL, DRV, OVL, SYS.

2 Log on to the directory that holds the text file.

3 Type the command:

TYPE *filename* **| MORE**

MORE displays a text file a screenful at a time - see later.

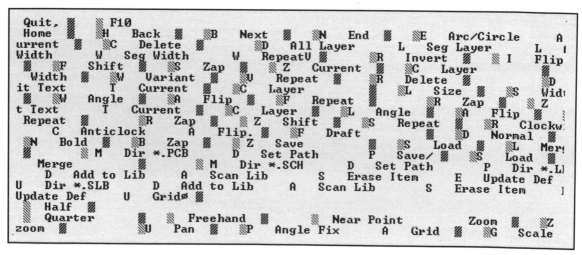

96

Viewing with TYPE

4 Read the first page of the file and press any key to progress to the next.

5 If you want to stop before the end of the file, press **[Ctrl]-[C]** to end the display.

MS-DOS has a command word TYPE that can be used to show the contents of a text file on the screen. You have seen COPY used for this purpose, but TYPE has some advantages over COPY in this respect.

TYPE, used with a short text file, will show the whole file on the screen. When the file is a long one, the screen scrolls, rolling the text upwards faster than you can read it. COPY filename CON does this too, but when you use TYPE you can get around the problem.

The example shows the effect of using:

TYPE *filename* | more

which will fill the screen, then wait for you to press a key before displaying the next set of lines of the file. Get into the habit of using the Spacebar or **[Enter]** when you are asked to use "any key".

```
TYPE README.TXT | MORE
This file contains information that is not available during the
printing of the manual. Please read all the sections before you
proceed with any installation procedure .

This file contains the following sections:

   1. SBTalker
      1.1 Installation
      1.2 Blaster Environment

   2. Monologue for Windows
      2.1 Version and Copyright
      2.2 Installation
      2.3 Configuration

   3. Software Package Listing

-- More --
```

press any key to continue

Viewing groups of files

TYPE will not accept a wildcard as its arguments, so you cannot use a line such as:

TYPE *.TXT

to display several files. There is a way round this, but it does not allow you to look at the files page by page in the way that **TYPE filename | MORE** does.

To use TYPE with a wildcard set of files, alter the command to:

FOR %A in (*.TXT) DO TYPE %A

which will, in this example, display all the TXT files in a directory - but will scroll all the way.

This FOR..IN..DO structure can be used with other commands, usually as a way of forcing them to accept a wildcard. It is seldom needed nowadays, and this example has been included only to point out that there is nearly always a way out of a problem. Nowadays there are usually other easier ways - like using DOSHELL.

1 You can stop scrolling using **[Ctrl]-[S]** and start it again using **[Ctrl]-[Q]**, but you need nimble fingers to stop and start at the right places.

2 If a file contains the **[Ctrl]-[Z]** character, ASCII code 31, TYPE will display nothing following it, because [Ctrl]-[Z] is used to mark the end of a text file.

Take note

Never use **TYPE** or **COPY** to send a program file to a printer - the effects are unpredictable (like running through all your paper).

T-control

☐ You can use [Page Up] and [Page Down] , as well as a set of other keys listed at the foot of the screen when T is running.

using the T utility with a text file

Viewing with T

When you use a TYPE command to look at text in a text file, you can't recall any of the file - you can only read down the text, not up again.

If you want to recall some of the text you need to repeat the TYPE command. The alternatives are to use a utility such as T.COM (a public-domain utility), or to use the F9 key with DOSSHELL.

The **T.COM** program is not part of MS-DOS, but it is so useful that many PC owners regard it as an essential. It can be obtained from any supplier of shareware or Public Domain utilities for only the cost of the disk.

The illustration below shows the use of the **T** command. The file in the display is one of the MS-DOS README files that is distributed with MS-DOS 6.0.

The advantage of a text **reader** like TYPE or T is that, unlike a text **editor**, there is no risk of altering the file.

```
T README.TXT
====================

This file provides important information not included in the
MICROSOFT MS-DOS 6 USER'S GUIDE or in MS-DOS Help.

This file is divided into the following major sections:

1. Setup
2. MemMaker, EMM386, and Memory Management
3. Windows
4. Hardware Compatibility with MS-DOS 6.2
5. Microsoft Programs
6. Third-Party Programs
7. DoubleSpace

If the subject you need information about doesn't appear in
this file, you might find it in one of the following text
files included with MS-DOS:

* OS2.TXT, which describes how to remove and save data on your
Command▶    *** Top of file ***         Options: h8kMpswTalj Keys: X=exit ?=▶
```

Pipes

Pipes and filters are a part of DOS that many PC owners never learn to use. That's their loss, because these items can make a lot of impossible-looking tasks quite easy to perform. They are particularly applicable to text files.

A **pipe** is a way of taking the output of an action somewhere else. For example, the output of the DIR command is normally always to the screen. By using a pipe, you can make the DIR information go to the printer directly, or to a file. The output of DIR is text, and that's why all this can be done.

The illustration below shows the output of a DIR command being piped to a file called *dirfil.txt*. This allows you to keep files of your directory contents, print them, and save them to a floppy. It's all very useful when the hard drive packs up.

❑ **To make DIR transfer its text into a file**

1 Log on to the directory whose listing you want to keep.

2 Type the command:

   DIR > dirfil.txt

   leaving a space each side of the chevron.

3 Press **[Enter]** and wait for the file to be created.

4 You can check the file using **TYPE**.

get to directory

pipe the DIR command

now check using TYPE

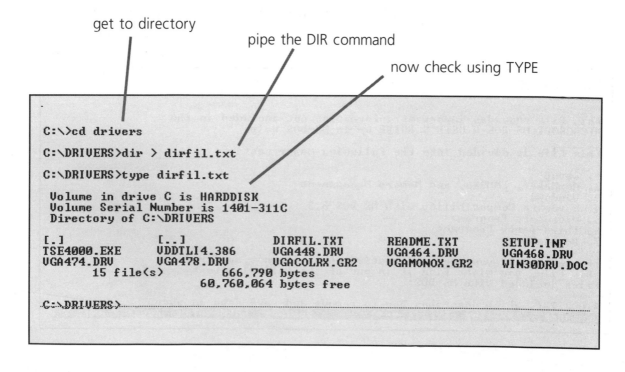

```
C:\>cd drivers

C:\DRIVERS>dir > dirfil.txt

C:\DRIVERS>type dirfil.txt

 Volume in drive C is HARDDISK
 Volume Serial Number is 1401-311C
 Directory of C:\DRIVERS

[.]             [..]              DIRFIL.TXT       README.TXT      SETUP.INF
TSE4000.EXE     VDDTLI4.386       VGA448.DRV       VGA464.DRV      VGA468.DRV
VGA474.DRV      VGA478.DRV        VGACOLRX.GR2     VGAMONOX.GR2    WIN30DRV.DOC
        15 file(s)           666,790 bytes
                          60,760,064 bytes free

C:\DRIVERS>
```

Filters

You can use :

DIR > PRN

to send the directory listing straight to the printer.

The double chevron **>>** appends text to an existing file. For example

DIR >> olddir.txt

will add the listing of the current directory to the olddir file.

When you make use of a pipe action, it's nearly always to make text that normally appears on screen go to the printer or to a file.

This is not the only use for a pipe, because you can transfer text in other ways. You can transfer text that comes out of a command or a program into another program. There are only a few programs that will accept text piped into them. These are specially written to allow it, and are called filters.

A **filter** is a program that has been written in a way that allows it to have its input piped as well as its output. Filter programs can usually be run as programs in their own right as well as being used to alter the output or input of another program.

The vertical bar symbol (|) is used to indicate connection to a filter - you can also pipe to or from a filter.

NOTE: When you pipe something that normally appears on the screen, there will be no screen display because it has been piped away.

Take note

Confine the use of the pipe to text files. The main exception is when the output of a word-processor has been put into a file, and this can later be piped to the printer.

SORTing text files

The SORT filter will take a text file, where each line is a separate item and sort it into (ASCII) alphabetical order

In the example below, a file of text has been prepared, using words that are not in order. By using the **SORT** filter following **TYPE**, the list is displayed in sorted order on the screen.

You can get the same action by piping the textfile to **SORT** using:

    SORT < TEST.TXT

with no need for using the **TYPE** command. You can remember this with the phrase *piping replaces typing*.

❑ Note the order of commands:

TYPE filename | FILTER

SORT is used in the example following **TYPE**, and with the | character (**[Shift]** - **[\]**) used as a form of connector.

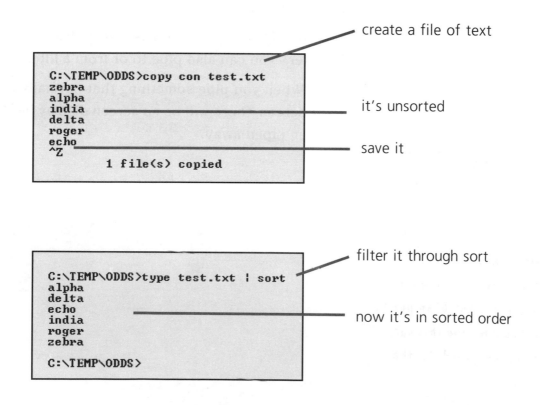

create a file of text

```
C:\TEMP\ODDS>copy con test.txt
zebra
alpha
india
delta
roger
echo
^Z
        1 file(s) copied
```

it's unsorted

save it

```
C:\TEMP\ODDS>type test.txt | sort
alpha
delta
echo
india
roger
zebra

C:\TEMP\ODDS>
```

filter it through sort

now it's in sorted order

Points

It's difficult to remember any kind of rules for these actions, and the best way to cope with them is by examples.

You can combine a filter and a piping action, but you need to think about it. For example, using:

TYPE A | SORT > B

will take the list of text from file A, sort it and save it as the file B.

Note: There are usually at least two ways of achieving any given result. You can very often use either the pipe symbol or the filter symbol, providing that you use each in the correct way.

Inputs and outputs

Suppose you have a file of words that you want to use in an index, so that they are not at the moment in alphabetical order. If the unsorted words are in a file called *unsort.txt* and you want them placed in order into a file called *index.txt*, you can use the command:

SORT < unsort.txt > index.txt

Notice the order here, because it is important. The SORT filter comes first, then the piping in sign and the unsorted file, then the piping out sign and the sorted file.

This is an example of SORT being used with only the pipe signs, not the filter connector sign.

The MORE filter

This can be used in the form:

MORE < textfile

and this will print the text of the file on the screen, pausing when the screen is full with the "More" message to indicate that pressing any key will continue the action. As we saw earlier, the alternative use is:

TYPE textfile | MORE

FINDing words in files

There is a FIND program in the MS-DOS collection which can be used as a program in its own right or as a filter. As the name suggests, it is used to find words in a text file. Its filter use can be very effective, saving you a considerable amount of effort.

Suppose you have in the directory you are logged to a file of text called *newtext.txt*, and you are looking for the word "computer" (happens to me all the time). You can use FIND in this way:

FIND "computer" newtext.txt

and you will see on the screen all the places in the file where this word has appeared.

The example below shows a search for the word "BIN" using a README file.

1 Log to the directory that holds the file you want to search.

2 Type **FIND** followed by the word or phrase you want to find, in quotes, then the name of the file.

3 If you want the lines to be numbered, add the parameter **/N**.

4 If you want to count the occurrences, add the parameter **/C**.

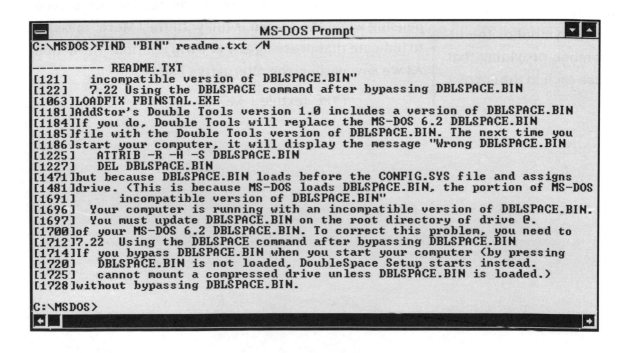

```
                              MS-DOS Prompt
C:\MSDOS>FIND "BIN" readme.txt /N

---------- README.TXT
[121]    incompatible version of DBLSPACE.BIN"
[122]    7.22 Using the DBLSPACE command after bypassing DBLSPACE.BIN
[1063]LOADFIX FBINSTAL.EXE
[1181]AddStor's Double Tools version 1.0 includes a version of DBLSPACE.BIN
[1184]If you do, Double Tools will replace the MS-DOS 6.2 DBLSPACE.BIN
[1185]file with the Double Tools version of DBLSPACE.BIN. The next time you
[1186]start your computer, it will display the message "Wrong DBLSPACE.BIN
[1225]    ATTRIB -R -H -S DBLSPACE.BIN
[1227]    DEL DBLSPACE.BIN
[1471]but because DBLSPACE.BIN loads before the CONFIG.SYS file and assigns
[1481]drive. (This is because MS-DOS loads DBLSPACE.BIN, the portion of MS-DOS
[1691]    incompatible version of DBLSPACE.BIN"
[1696]  Your computer is running with an incompatible version of DBLSPACE.BIN.
[1697]  You must update DBLSPACE.BIN on the root directory of drive C.
[1700]of your MS-DOS 6.2 DBLSPACE.BIN. To correct this problem, you need to
[1712]7.22  Using the DBLSPACE command after bypassing DBLSPACE.BIN
[1714]If you bypass DBLSPACE.BIN when you start your computer (by pressing
[1720]    DBLSPACE.BIN is not loaded, DoubleSpace Setup starts instead.
[1725]    cannot mount a compressed drive unless DBLSPACE.BIN is loaded.)
[1728]without bypassing DBLSPACE.BIN.

C:\MSDOS>
```

5 Use the parameter **/I** to make the search case-insensitive. Without **/I**, searching for "Brown" will not find "brown". With it, these words are treated as being identical.

6 Press **[Enter]** to start the action.

In the example, the lines of the file have been numbered to make it easier to locate them. This is done by adding the parameter **/N** which will show the number of each line in which the word is found. Using **/C** would show how many times the word had occurred, but not where.

FIND can be used as a very useful filter. Suppose, for example, you wanted to find which files in a directory were created in the year 1991. Find can help - but there is a snag - see below:

use these only if your normal DIR gives a **w**ide listing, **p**ausing when the screen is full

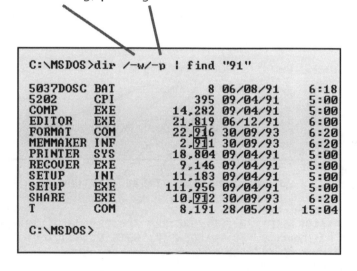

```
C:\MSDOS>dir /-w/-p | find "91"

5037DOSC BAT            8  06/08/91     6:18
5202     CPI          395  09/04/91     5:00
COMP     EXE       14,282  09/04/91     5:00
EDITOR   EXE       21,819  06/12/91     6:00
FORMAT   COM       22,916  30/09/93     6:20
MEMMAKER INF        2,911  30/09/93     6:20
PRINTER  SYS       18,804  09/04/91     5:00
RECOVER  EXE        9,146  09/04/91     5:00
SETUP    INI       11,183  09/04/91     5:00
SETUP    EXE      111,956  09/04/91     5:00
SHARE    EXE       10,912  30/09/93     6:20
T        COM        8,191  28/05/91    15:04

C:\MSDOS>
```

The years 1991 have been found, but so also have files whose sizes happened to include the figures *91*. The moral is that it would be better to search for "*/91*" because this combination is found only in the dates.

Dumping output

Finally, there's a dump for words you don't want, called NUL (it's classed as a device, like PRN and CON). If you have a program that starts by printing on the screen a lot of information that you don't want, you can make the unwanted words invisible.

Suppose, for example, that you have a program called BRAG.EXE which prints a screen full of information each time you start it running. Usually, if you run the program using the line:

BRAG > NUL

you can avoid this. The example below shows this being used in a set of commands from an AUTOEXEC.BAT file.

❑ If you use the NUL device to dump unwanted text, remember that you have used it. You may at some time later wonder why you do not get any "signing-on" message from a program.

❑ You cannot get rid of all program messages by using NUL, only the ones that appear while the program is loading.

dump the screen messages from these

```
@ECHO OFF
loadhigh C:\MSDOS\SHARE.EXE /l:500 \f:5100
SET BLASTER=A220 I5 D1 H5 P330 T6 > NUL
SET SOUND=C:\SB16
C:\SB16\SB16SET /M:220 /VOC:220 /CD:220 /MIDI:220 /LINE:220 /TREBLE:0 > NUL
PATH C:\MSDOS;C:\;C:\WINDOWS;C:\BATS;C:\monologw > NUL
set dircmd=/w/p/o:gn
set temp=c:\temp
C:\SB16\SBCONFIG.EXE /S > NUL
C:\MSDOS\doskey/insert
LH /L:1,56928 C:\WINDOWS\mouse.COM /Y > NUL
C:\MSDOS\keyb uk,,C:\msdos\keyboard.sys
LH /L:1,640 keyclick
C:\msdos\MSCDEX.EXE /D:MSCD000  /M:16
C:\MSDOS\smartdrv /x
rem C:\scrngrab\pinch\pinch c:\temp
win
```

Finding files in DOSSHELL

As you might expect by now, you can carry out these file searches more easily with DOSSHELL. This is because you can arrange to have your files listed in order of date, allowing you to pick out all the ones for the year you are interested in.

The illustration below shows DOSSHELL displaying a list of files in date order:

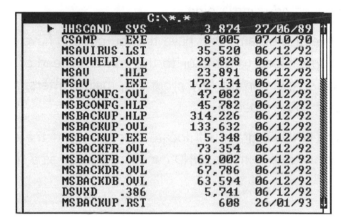

A list like this makes it easy to pick out files of the date that you want.

Take Note!

The File Display Options in DOSSHELL let you sort in order of Name, Extension, Date, Size and DIskOrder — and either ascending or descending

Summary

- [ ] Text files use ASCII codes, and contain readable text laid out in lines, with no strange characters. This distinguishes them from program files.

- [ ] Text files can be read on the screen by using the **TYPE** command, and you can filter this through **MORE** if you want to view a long text page by page.

- [ ] You can use the **SORT** filter to arrange a list of words or phrases into alphabetical order. This filter can be connected using a **pipe**.

- [ ] Several programs that have text output can have the output piped to a file or to the printer instead of to the screen. Only a few programs, mainly **filters**, allow text to be piped in.

- [ ] The **FIND** program will locate text for you if the text occurs in a text file. FIND can also be used as a filter.

10 PRINT and EDIT

PRINTing files

PRINT will, as the name suggests, print a text file on paper. You must have the printer connected, switched on, and on line. If you think that advice is too obvious you have never manned a computer retailer's help line.

PRINT is, however, not as simple as you might expect. For one thing, it is a program that will sit in the memory working away while you get on with other things. That type of program is called a background program, and PRINT is one of a very few that you are likely to have.

This harks back to the days when printers were very slow, and you might need to wait several hours for a long document to be printed. Using PRINT avoids the computer being tied up while all this is going on.

1 Log on to the directory that holds the text files, or make a note of the path and filename for each if they are in different directories.

2 Type **PRINT** and follow it with the filenames, up to a limit of ten. Leave a space between each.

3 When you press **[Enter]** you will be asked to confirm that your printer is the device called PRN. For 99% of us, it is.

start work

message

```
PRINT C:\MSDOS\TEST2.TXT

Resident part of PRINT installed

  C:\MSDOS\TEST2.TXT is currently being printed
C:\MSDOS>

C:\MSDOS>print

Errors on list device indicate that it
may be off-line. Please check it.

  C:\MSDOS\TEST2.TXT is currently being printed


C:\MSDOS>print
PRINT queue is empty
```

can use any other commands

check to see what's happening

didn't switch it on!

all done

110

4 PRINT will churn away at the files until they are all printed, or you type **PRINT /T** to remove all the remaining files from the queue.

❏ The fact that PRINT can run in the background can make it very useful.

❏ Its limitations are that it will print the files exactly as they are. If you prepared the files on an editor set to 135 characters per line, and your printer is set for 80 you'll be sorry.

PRINT can be supplied with a list of files and left to get on with it while you use your brains more productively.

If your printer is switched off, PRINT will wait for you to switch it on. This is illustrated in the lines of the illustration opposite. If you are using other programs while PRINT churns away, you can type, while you are between programs:

    PRINT

and get a report on the progress of PRINT. This will tell you how many files remain to be printed (the print queue) and if any problems have arisen.

In the early days of DOS, PRINT was used extensively to make hard (printed) copy of text. Nowadays we are more likely to use Text Editor or word-processor programs for this task, and the printing commands in these programs take care of printing the text files.

Nevertheless, not many of these will allow you to get on with other things while the files are printed, and if you have a long file and a slow printer, PRINT can be useful.

Take note

You cannot use a file prepared by a word-processor unless it has been saved in ASCII form with line breaks. All major word-processors can provide files in this form.

Printing to file

A file that has been prepared by a word-processor in strict ASCII form will contain none of the effects that you can obtain with a word-processor, such as bold or italic print, changes of margins and so on.

You can print using the effects only if you use the Print to File output of the word processor.

To make a suitable file, instruct your-processor to **Print to File**. Provide a filename, and when you are ready, use **PRINT** on the file.

In general, however, if a word-processor has prepared a file of text, you should also use that same word-processor to print it. Use PRINT only for exceptional cases, and for text files that you know are in strictly ASCII form.

1 Instruct your word-processor to **Print to File**.

2 Provide a filename, and wait for the file to be created. This may take some time, particularly on a floppy disk

3 Later, you can use the **PRINT** command on this file, when the printer is on line.

Tip

Using Print to File and PRINT makes it possible to prepare document for printing on another machine. As long as the machine that is connected to the printer can read your file, the printing will be carried out.

Print hints

PRINT can take some parameters when you first use it in a session - you have to reset these each time you switch on if you want to alter the built-in defaults. Most users can work with the default values, but you might possibly want to work with a queue of up to 20 items, for example, by using /Q:20. Once you have used these parameters you can't alter the values unless you switch off and reboot.

The other parameters are noted below, but in general you should leave these alone unless you are certain that altering a parameter will help you. Using a larger buffer value can be useful to make printing more continuous, but if you use too much memory in this way you may find that you cannot run other programs for lack of memory.

Take note

You can use the COPY filename PRN command line as an alternative to PRINT, but remember that it can cope with one file only.

PARAMETER and defaults	Use
/B:512	set amount of memory used by PRINT. Use multiples of 512 here.
/D:LPT1	declare printer port. You might use LPT2.
/Q:10	queue holds 10 items. You may want more
/S:8	1/8 of computer's time is used for printing

Introducing EDIT

You can create and edit text using the built-in Editor of MS-DOS, and this can be used to ensure that your text is in purely ASCII code form.

The Editor of modern MS-DOS versions (MS-DOS 5.0 onwards) is a part of the QBasic program that is stored with the other MS-DOS utilities. QBasic is a type of program called an interpreter, which allows you to write your own programs, using a text file.

If you have deleted QBASIC in the belief that you would never need it, you will have deleted the Editor as well. You will need to replace QBASIC.EXE (though not QBASIC.HLP) and EDIT.COM. to get back the use of the Editor.

1 Log on to where the MS-DOS files are stored - check by using **DIR** that you have the files called *EDIT.COM* and *QBASIC.EXE*.

2 Type:

   EDIT [Enter]

3 When the EDIT introductory screen appears, press **[Enter]** to see the guide, or **[Esc]** to start editing.

4 The guide tells you how to get Help, and how to use the menu items.

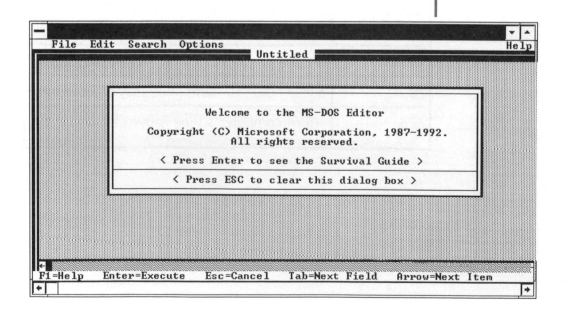

EDIT File commands

New is used when you have saved a file and want to start a new, un-named, one.

Open is used to edit an existing file - you'll see a list of directories and files when you use this.

Save As is used to save a file you have just created, or to save an existing file under a new name.

Save is used for a file which already has a name and has been edited.

Take note

Using the Editor is much simpler if you have a mouse.

If you don't, you use the Alt key to highlight the menu items, and then press the highlighted letter to start the menu.

When you use the command EDIT you will see the opening screen of the Editor, opposite. This allows you to press **[Enter]** to see a brief guide, or to press **[ESC]** to start editing right away.

The **File** menu is illustrated below. To open it, use **[Alt]**, then **[F]**, or click with the mouse on the word **File**.

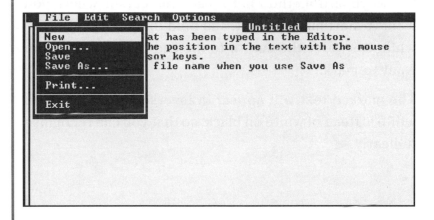

When you start EDIT with no file to read, you can type whatever text you want, using the normal letter and number keys.

When you have prepared your text, select the **File** menu, followed by the **Save As** item. You will be asked to provide a filename, following the usual rules on filenames.

You should use the extension of *TXT* on your text file unless you need to use some other extension, such as *BAT* for a batch file.

Editing Text

The Edit menu can be used by pressing **[Alt]** and then **[E]**. The mouse alternative is to click on the word **Edit**. The items in this menu cannot be used unless you have first marked out the text you want to edit in this way.

Text can be marked using the mouse by dragging the cursor across the text with the mouse button held down. The keyboard method is to place the cursor where you want to start marking text, and hold the **[Shift]** key down while you move the cursor to the end of the section you want to mark.

The marked text will appear in inverse video, black on white instead of white on black, so that you can recognise it clearly.

marked text

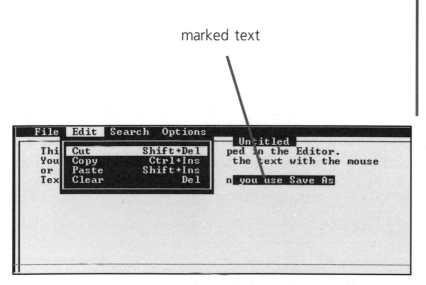

The Edit menu

Cut will make the text disappear. The text is, in fact, stored temporarily in a piece of memory called the *Clipboard*. It will remain there until you use Cut or Copy again.

Copy will also copy the text to the Clipboard, but the text remains in place in the file

Paste will insert Cut or Copied text, wherever the cursor is when you use the command.

Clear will delete the marked text without storing it in the Clip-board.

The Search menu

Find will seek out any given word or phrase in the text that you are editing.

Repeat Find is used to find the next occurrence of the same word of phrase.

Change can be used to alter the found word or phrase to something else. It will work through all of the text, making these replacements.

The Options menu

allows you to select the colours to use for text and background.

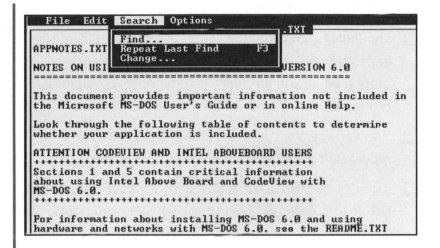

Printing

When you have edited and saved text, you can print it. Check that the printer is on line, and select the **File** menu and then the **Print** item. The text that is loaded into the Editor will be printed.

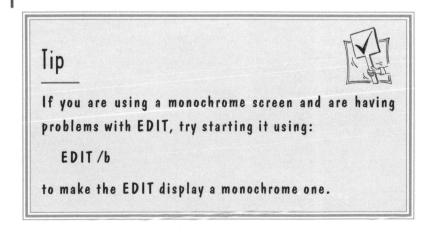

Tip

If you are using a monochrome screen and are having problems with EDIT, try starting it using:

EDIT /b

to make the EDIT display a monochrome one.

Summary

❑ The **PRINT** command will set up a queue of files waiting to be printed, and will print them in the background while you are running some other program or programs.

❑ You can use the command **PRINT** at intervals to get a report on how PRINT is coping with its queue

❑ You call up the QBasic Editor with the **EDIT** command. Use it to create text files to use as your own notes, or for batch files (see Section 12). You can also use the Editor to read text files.

❑ The Editor has some of the facilities of a word-processor, allowing you to find words or phrases and, if required, replace them with others.

11 Time and Date

Setting the clock

The PC hardware, with a little help from MS-DOS, maintains a record of time and date, and will code both of these items into each file that is created and saved.

Though the date portion of this information is usually kept accurately, the same cannot be said about time. The PC is no Rolex and no Swatch. It isn't as valuable as a Rolex, and it certainly can't keep time like a Swatch.

This might seem odd when you know that the PC uses timing crystals that are just as precise as the types that are fitted in modern watches.

The illustration below shows how a TIME check is carried out, and time corrected.

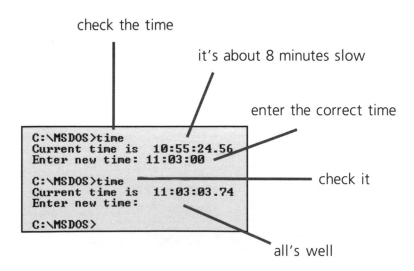

check the time

it's about 8 minutes slow

enter the correct time

```
C:\MSDOS>time
Current time is  10:55:24.56
Enter new time: 11:03:00

C:\MSDOS>time
Current time is  11:03:03.74
Enter new time:

C:\MSDOS>
```

check it

all's well

Basic steps

1 Log on to the directory that holds the MS-DOS utility files, unless you have a PATH line set up.

2 Type

   TIME

   You will see the time in HH:MM:SS form, with a line inviting you to enter the new time figure.

3 Enter the correct time at the prompt – set it to the nearest whole minute.

4 Press **[Enter]**, and use **TIME** again to check. If it is OK, just press **[Enter]**.

❑ The TIME command will accept the letters a for AM or p for PM. For example, 2:44 pm can be entered as:

   14:44 or

   2:44p

120

Basic steps

1 Log on to the correct directory, unless you have a PATH line.

2 Type

    DATE [Enter]

3 Type a new date if required, otherwise just press **[Enter]**.

❏ You can type the date using dots, hyphens or slashmarks to separate the items. The examples below are all valid:

    12.4.94

    12-4-94

    12/4/94

DATE will reject an impossible date such as 31/2/94.

Setting the date

Some very old PC models required you to enter the date and time whenever you switched them on. This has not been necessary for a long time now, and if your machine suddenly requests you to fill in this information, it is likely that the battery is defective.

One of the timing crystals in your PC is used for computing work, but it stops when the PC is switched off. The other is operated by a battery, and its counting action can be interrupted at times. It's the interruption that cause mis-counting, so that the time you read on the PC is nearly always slow.

The date is checked and adjusted in much the same way as time, using **DATE** and typing a new date if needed.

get the date

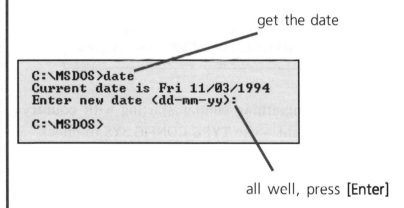

```
C:\MSDOS>date
Current date is Fri 11/03/1994
Enter new date (dd-mm-yy):

C:\MSDOS>
```

all well, press **[Enter]**

The date is normally precise - but if you find you need to correct it, this might be a sign of battery trouble.

Inside Information

If you find that the time or, more usually the date, are in a format that you are not used to, like Month - Day - Year, then the cause is that your PC is not set up correctly. Find who did it.

There is a file called CONFIG.SYS, see later, which determines this. If you do not have the line illustrated below in your CONFIG.SYS file, your computer will use the USA settings. The UK settings are set by the number 044 that appears in the illustration (right). This is (intentionally) the international telephone prefix number for dialling to the UK from abroad.

Remember that this is just one line among several - you will have to look for it.

```
country=044,850,C:\MSDOS\country.sy
```

This line, or something similar starting with **country=** should be present – use **TYPE CONFIG.SYS** to check.

CMOS RAM

❑ The battery also keeps a small piece of memory active. This memory is called the CMOS RAM.

❑ The CMOS RAM holds information on the disk drives (hard and floppy) as well as the date and time information.

❑ If the battery is at the end of its life you can get odd-looking error messages, such as being unable to find the floppy drive. Worse still, you may find that you cannot boot from the hard drive.

❑ If all the information in the CMOS RAM memory has been lost, the machine will have to be set up again after a new battery has been fitted.

Daily TIME checks

If you use any program that has an alarm facility, setting off a sound beeper when a preset time is reached, you need to keep the time reasonably precise. For a machine that is used daily, you may need to correct the time daily.

If you need this, add the line:

    TIME

to your AUTOEXEC.BAT file (see Section 13). This will prompt you to type the correct time when you boot the computer, and it will ensure that the clock is reasonably precise for that day.

Finally, remember that files keep the date and time information of the instant when they were originally saved. If you want to alter this, look back at the COPY command in the form:

    COPY file+,, newname

which will change the date and time information on the copy to that of the time when the COPY action was carried out.

Take Note!

If you didn't know there was a battery in your PC, you know now. It is usually a long-life Silver Oxide or Lithium type and is soldered on the motherboard. Replacing it requires soldering skills. Some PCs use a mains+battery supply which plugs into the motherboard. Many users replace their computers before the battery gives out.

Summary

❏ The PC keeps track of time and date by using a clock chip which, along with a small portion of memory, is maintained by a battery when the machine is switched off.

❏ The date is usually kept correct, but the time can often be slow because the clock count can be interrupted by other PC actions.

❏ The MS-DOS commands **DATE** and **TIME** can be used to look at what is currently being used and to correct it if necessary.

❏ The date and time are noted with every data file that you save, but if you use the **COPY** command with its **+,,** addition, you can change the date and time for a copy.

❏ Trouble with the date usually points to a battery at the end of its life, and this will cause other problems (such as the hard drive no longer being available). Some boards allow an external battery to be used - but you need to consult someone with hardware experience.

12 Batch files

Automation!

Picture this. You use every day a program called WORDCHOP. Before you can use it, you need to log on to the directory C:\WORDS\TEXT\EDITORS and you need to run a short utility called SETPRINT before you type WORDCHOP to start your program. Tedious, isn't it?

What would you give for some way of making all these steps run automatically? You needn't give anything because it's all present in MS-DOS, using batch files.

A batch file is a text file - which means that you can create it using EDIT, and you can view it using TYPE.

Here's a batch file that has been written and has just been named so that the file can be saved, using EDIT.

your batch file lines

the SAVE AS dialog box

drive/directory choice

Basic steps

1 Start **EDIT**, and type in the lines as shown in the illustration .

2 Take a new line for each, using **[Enter]**.

3 When you have done, use the **File** menu and select **Save As**.

4 For the file name type **ALPHA.BAT** and then move the cursor to the **OK** button and press **[Enter]** (or click with the mouse).

5 You can now carry out these command lines by typing

    ALPHA   [Enter]

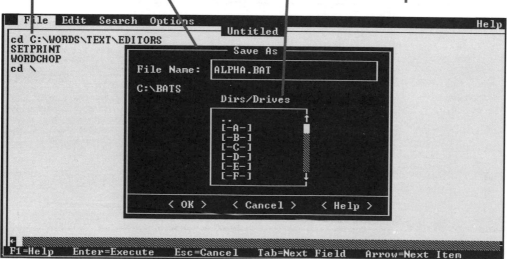

```
  File  Edit  Search  Options                              Help
                              Untitled
cd C:\WORDS\TEXT\EDITORS
SETPRINT                  ── Save As ──
WORDCHOP
cd \           File Name:  ALPHA.BAT

               C:\BATS
                          Dirs/Drives

                          ..
                          [-A-]
                          [-B-]
                          [-C-]
                          [-D-]
                          [-E-]
                          [-F-]

                  < OK >    < Cancel >    < Help >


F1=Help    Enter=Execute    Esc=Cancel    Tab=Next Field    Arrow=Next Item
```

A batch file must..

- [ ] be a text file whose name has the extension letters of BAT.

- [ ] have each command on a separate line

- [ ] be created by a text editor, or saved as an ASCII text file from a word-processor.

The batch file contains only the commands that you would normally type, and it is saved using a name of your choice with the extension (very important) of BAT. That's all. Now if you named your file ALPHA.BAT, then all you need to do to carry out the steps above to run your WORDCHOP program is to type ALPHA and press ENTER.

That assumes, of course, that you are logged to the directory that contains the batch file ALPHA.BAT, or that the path to the batch file is established, see later.

How many times, when you have to type a long path to a directory, do you mis-spell the name of one directory, or type the bar | instead of the slash \? Using a batch file, you need to get it perfect just once and once only.

A BATS directory

Your use of batch files is greatly eased if you keep all of them, except AUTOEXEC.BAT, in a separate directory called, for example, BATS.

One such collection is illustrated below.

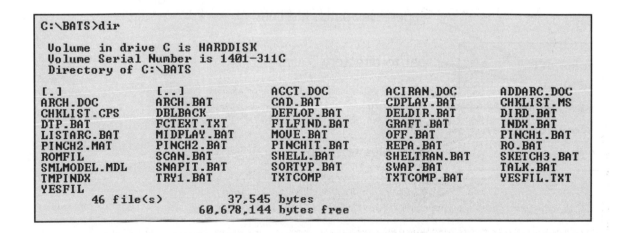

```
C:\BATS>dir
 Volume in drive C is HARDDISK
 Volume Serial Number is 1401-311C
 Directory of C:\BATS

[.]              [..]             ACCT.DOC         ACIRAN.DOC       ADDARC.DOC
ARCH.DOC         ARCH.BAT         CAD.BAT          CDPLAY.BAT       CHKLIST.MS
CHKLIST.CPS      DBLBACK          DEFLOP.BAT       DELDIR.BAT       DIRD.BAT
DTP.BAT          FCTEXT.TXT       FILFIND.BAT      GRAFT.BAT        INDX.BAT
LISTARC.BAT      MIDPLAY.BAT      MOVE.BAT         OFF.BAT          PINCH1.BAT
PINCH2.MAT       PINCH2.BAT       PINCHIT.BAT      REPA.BAT         RO.BAT
ROMFIL           SCAN.BAT         SHELL.BAT        SHELTRAN.BAT     SKETCH3.BAT
SMLMODEL.MDL     SNAPIT.BAT       SORTYP.BAT       SWAP.BAT         TALK.BAT
TMPINDX          TRY1.BAT         TXTCOMP          TXTCOMP.BAT      YESFIL.TXT
YESFIL
        46 file(s)         37,545 bytes
                      60,678,144 bytes free
```

BATs in belfries

A whole cave-full of bats, 46 in all, fit into just over 37 Kbyte of space in the C:\BAT directory illustrated on the previous page. It's a lot of action in a small space.

The illustration below shows one of these files. It is intended to run a CAD program, and it includes a line that will save any new or altered files to a floppy in drive A:. It also has a line ECHO OFF that prevents the lines of the batch file from appearing on the screen.

There are only five lines to this batch file, which is typical of the type of batch files you can write for yourself. These five lines, however, are lines that you would otherwise have to type, and type perfectly, each time you wanted to run this program. The lines have been spaced out in this view so as to make the comments clear.

The words you use in a batch file, like those in command lines, can be in upper or lower case.

How it works

1 The line **ECHO OFF** prevents the batch commands being shown on the screen.

2 **CD\DRAW** gets to the correct directory for this example.

3 **BIGCAD** is the command that runs this (imaginary) CAD program from the C:\DRAW directory.

4 **XCOPY C: A: /n** is a command that will save to the floppy in A: any data files that have been changed - it's an automatic backup.

5 **CD** returns to the root directory.

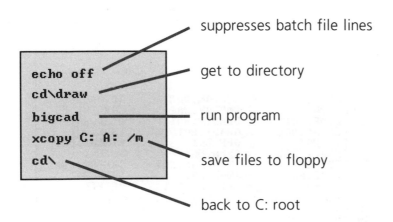

```
echo off          suppresses batch file lines
cd\draw           get to directory
bigcad            run program
xcopy C: A: /m    save files to floppy
cd\               back to C: root
```

128

Parameters

❏ Some programs need parameters. Suppose that when you run one called WRITENOW you add a name for the data file it will use, with a line like:

WRITENOW MYDAT

❏ How is this dealt with when WRITENOW is started by a batch file? The answer is that any parameters can be written after the batch file name, just as they can after the program name.

❏ In the example, a batch file called W.BAT could then be run by typing:

W MYDAT

When a batch file runs, it does exactly the same actions as would be done when you typed each command and pressed [Enter], in the sequence that you have put into the batch file.

That means, of course, that the text of each line will appear on the screen as it is carried out. Using **ECHO OFF** suppresses this - but not the first line that consists of ECHO OFF. You can suppress even this one by using the at (@) sign in the form: **@ECHO OFF.**

If any of the lines in the file cause unwanted messages on the screen, you can suppress these by piping them to **NUL**, as shown earlier using **> NUL** after the command. This will not conceal any important messages, like error messages, but it will prevent the screen starting to look like a Christmas list.

Here's a batch file that discards signing-on messages. It also loads a utility program into the memory, runs the main program, and then removes the utility. This type of action is quite often needed.

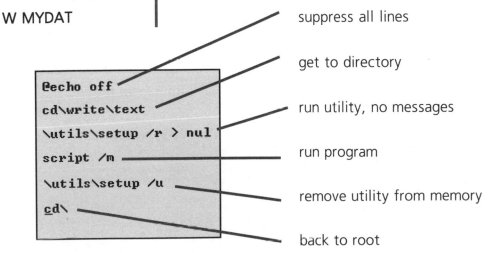

```
@echo off
cd\write\text
\utils\setup /r > nul
script /m
\utils\setup /u
cd\
```

suppress all lines

get to directory

run utility, no messages

run program

remove utility from memory

back to root

Parameters for BATS

The %1 parameter

The example below shows an indexing batch file that uses an imaginary text-editor called SHRDLU. By using the %1 parameter, you can supply a name when you call INDX, and this is the name that will be used for the sorted file.

If you need more than one parameter or argument, you can use %2, %3 and so on up to %9. You are not likely to need more than three of these parameters.

You can use a parameter like %1 more than once in a batch file - everywhere that you would expect to use whatever would be typed in place of %1 if you were running the program manually.

Example: typing **INDX sortfile.txt** will allow you to enter words and numbers until you quit SHRDLU. The file from this is saved with the temporary name *tmpind*. It is sorted and saved as *sortfile.txt*. This file is then passed to the editor. When you have finished editing it (by quitting SHRDLU), the batch file ends.

The way that a parameter is passed into a batch file is by using a parameter symbol, typically %1. If the batch file is called W.BAT and it contains the command:

> **WRITENOW %1**

then when you use the batch file you would type:

> **W MYDAT**

so that the name MYDAT would be used in place of the marker %1.

This form of use allows you to create batch files for programs that need an argument, and it can also be used when you need to specify parameters.

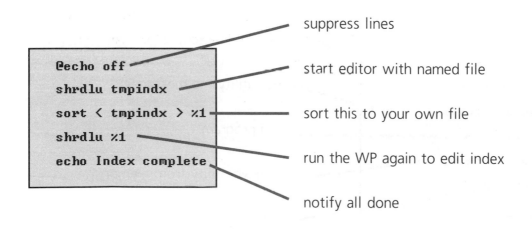

```
@echo off            ──────  suppress lines
shrdlu tmpindx       ──────  start editor with named file
sort < tmpindx > %1  ──────  sort this to your own file
shrdlu %1            ──────  run the WP again to edit index
echo Index complete  ──────  notify all done
```

- One point you need to watch is that if a batch file calls for an argument and you do not supply a name when you use the batch file all sorts of mayhem can result.

- There are ways of getting round this - but this is a **Made Simple** book, not a text for advanced users.

- The principle is to test that a name has been typed, and to leave the batch file if it has not.

Batch files are so useful that you might expect there would be a bookshelf full of texts about them. In fact there are only a few, and a lot of them are aimed at fairly expert users. You will find more about batch files in my *Newnes MS-DOS 6.0 Pocket Book*, published by Butterworth-Heinemann, and a great deal more in *User-Friendly Batch Files*, by Barry Coleman, published by Kuma Books.

Even if you never intend to write a batch file, you still need to know something about them, because your computer uses the one called AUTOEXEC.BAT to set up programs that are essential to its purposes.

The sort of lines that get into AUTOEXEC.BAT are covered in Section 13, and you need to know how and why these are used. You may also need to change them. particularly when you install a new program.

Meantime, think how you could use batch files. Do you need to run programs always in the same sequence? Put the commands in a batch file and run the batch file. Do you have problems remembering directory names for programs? Put them in a batch file and never trouble your memory again. Do you always forget that your favourite program needs a driver loaded before you can start it?. You know the answer by now.

Summary

❑ Batch files are text files of MS-DOS commands, arranged one line per command.

❑ Each batch file is saved with a short and memorable filename which must use the extension **BAT**.

❑ The use of batch file is made much easier if you keep them all in a separate directory such as C:\BATS, whose path is declared in a **PATH** line, see Section 13.

❑ A batch file is run by typing its name, just as if it were a program.

❑ You can pass an argument to a batch file in the same way as you pass the argument to a program, if the line that calls the program uses a parameter such as **%1**.

❑ The most important batch file is **AUTOEXEC.BAT**, because this file runs automatically when the computer is switched on.

13 The Start-Up Files

AUTOEXEC.BAT

Take a look at your AUTOEXEC.BAT file. Unless you have set up the computer for yourself, it will be very much as the supplier of your PC set it up. That might not be absolutely ideal for you.

In addition, programs nowadays come with SETUP or INSTALL actions that carry out the work of creating directories and copying files into them. These actions very often also make changes to AUTOEXEC.BAT.

Some SETUP programs notify you about these changes, others do not. In a few cases, the changes that are made can cause problems, and you need to sort them out for yourself.

The illustration shows a very simple batch file for a 386 machine:

command to view file

```
C:\WINDOWS>type C:\autoexec.bat

@ECHO OFF
PATH C:\MSDOS;C:\;C:\WINDOWS;C:\BATS
set dircmd=/w/p/o:gn
set temp=c:\temp
C:\MSDOS\doskey/insert
C:\MSDOS\mouse.COM /Y > NUL
C:\MSDOS\keyb uk,,C:\msdos\keyboard.sys
```

❏ To look at your AUTOEXEC.BAT file.

1 Log to the C:\ directory.

2 Use either

  TYPE AUTOEXEC.BAT

  or

COPY AUTOEXEC.BAT CON

  or

  EDIT AUTOEXEC.BAT

❏ The first two methods allow only viewing of the file, but **EDIT** also allows you to change the file.

The lines in this AUTOEXEC.BAT are explained in the next three pages.

The PATH line

☐ Each directory to be searched is listed.

☐ The semicolon is used to separate directory paths

☐ Don't make the PATH too long, otherwise too much time can be spent searching.

The PATH line that is shown contains as much as most users need. Some programs will add to this when they are installed - Windows, for example, always add the entry **C:\WINDOWS** to the PATH line.

Now take these lines one by one, following **@ECHO OFF** which prevents the lines themselves from appearing.

The **PATH** line is very important. It consists of a list of directories which will be searched when you type a program name without providing a path.

The normal action, with no PATH line, is to look for the program file in the directory you are using and, if it is not there, in the root directory of the drive you are using. After that, the search ends and you get an error message of the **Not Found** type.

In the example, the directories to be searched following the current one are the C:\MSDOS directory (where all the MSDOS utilities are stored for this machine), the C:\ root directory, and then the C:\BATS directory (to get the batch files).

You must have an entry that allows you quick access to your MS-DOS utilities (the external commands). MS-DOS versions from 5.0 onwards created your PATH line for you and also stored the MS-DOS files in a directory called either MSDOS or DOS.

Take note

You will get an error message if you specify in the **PATH** line a directory that does not exist.

SET

Lines that start with SET are often placed in AUTOEXEC.BAT or other batch file. SET is followed by a word called a *variable name*, which is used rather like a filename. This is followed by an equals sign, then some other item, often a directory name.

Take the **SET TEMP=C:\TEMP** example. This allows programs to make use of the word TEMP to mean a place to put temporary files. The program does not create a directory or even name one, it just uses the word TEMP, and the directory is named by the SET line in the AUTOEXEC.BAT file.

This gives you the freedom to use whatever directory you like, such as G:\BITS - the directory is created and named by you, not by the program.

Sound programs can use the word BLASTER to set these parameters ..

```
SET BLASTER=A220 I5 D1 H5 P330 T6 > NUL
```

..and use SOUND to mean this directory

```
SET SOUND=C:\SB16
```
DIRCMD carries the parameters for DIR

```
set dircmd=/w/p/o:gn
```
TEMP is a path for temporary files

```
set temp=c:\temp
```

Examples

SET TEMP=C:\TEMP is the most common example. This allows programs to make use of a **C:\TEMP** directory for the temporary files they create and destroy.

SET DIRCMD uses the word **DIRCMD** to carry information on parameters for the **DIR** command. By using a SET DIRCMD line you can force the DIR command, used without parameters, to work the way you want.

In the example, it creates a wide directory listing (**/W**), pausing after each screenful (**/P**) with names sorted alphabetically (**/O:N**), directories first (**\O:G**).

Memmaker

☐ **LOADHI** (or **LH**) lines in AUTOEXEC.BAT can be put in automatically if you use MS-DOS 6.0 or above.

1 Edit the AUTOEXEC.BAT file so that it contains all that you need.

2 Run the **MEMMAKER** program, from the MSDOS directory.

3 Leave it to alter your AUTOEXEC.BAT file automatically, placing as many resident programs as possible into "spare" (high) memory.

4 If the computer does not work correctly afterwards, MEMMAKER will automatically start again, and be more careful about its settings.

Memory resident programs

Other commands in AUTOEXEC.BAT run programs that are of the resident type. For example, the program called **MOUSE.COM** will make the mouse work. It would be pointless if the mouse worked only until you ran another program, so the mouse program stays in the memory until you switch off.

There are several programs like this, called TSR programs, all of which take up valuable memory. Modern machines can use a command **LOADHI** in these AUTOEXEC.BAT lines so that these programs are placed in memory that is not otherwise used, leaving the normal memory clear for your own programs. (See left column.)

The **KEYB** program is another example. It sets up the type of keyboard you are using - in this case for UK use rather than for US or for any other country. Keyboards for other countries follow the pattern of typewriter keyboards. For example, the US keyboard does not have the £ sign, and some other keys are differently arranged.

DOSKEY, the other program run by this AUTOEXEC.BAT, is a memory-resident utility that stores the commands you type in, and lets you recall and edit previous commands with the arrow cursor keys.

Take note

PATH and **SET** are commands that are used mainly in the AUTOEXEC.BAT file, though they can be used elsewhere.

CONFIG.SYS

Points

AUTOEXEC.BAT sets up resident programs, the PATH line and SET quantities for you when MS-DOS is loaded. There is another configuration file called CONFIG.SYS.

This is not a batch file, and it does not contain familiar MS-DOS command words. Its purpose is to see to actions that must be carried out before MS-DOS can take effect.

You cannot run CONFIG.SYS except by booting the computer. If you make changes to the file, they have no effect until you boot again.

These are illustrated below. This shows a simple CONFIG.SYS file for a 386 machine, for which the most important lines are the ones that start with COUNTRY and SHELL. If these are not correct, you will have endless problems.

```
DEVICE=C:\MSDOS\SETVER.EXE
DEVICE=C:\MSDOS\HIMEM.SYS
buffers=25
files=35

DOS=HIGH

country=044,850,C:\MSDOS\country.sys

SHELL=C:\MSDOS\COMMAND.COM C:\MSDOS\    /p

STACKS=9,512
```

1 The first **DEVICE** line sets up a program that over-rules program restrictions on DOS version (some programs would otherwise not run under any version of MS-DOS above 5.0).

2 The second sets up **HIMEM.SYS.** This prepares for use of extended memory, and must be active before anything tries to use that memory.

3 The **BUFFERS** and **FILES** lines set up pieces of memory for temporary use when handling files. Some programs need a large number of these in order to run efficiently.

4 **DOS=HIGH** puts COMMAND.COM into "spare" memory, so releasing more of the main memory for programs.

5 The **COUNTRY** line sets up UK conventions. Dates will be in DD-MM-YY form rather than in MM-DD-YY, and the £ sign can be used.

6 The **SHELL** line tells the PC to use COMMAND.COM, and indicates the directory for the MS-DOS files. The r **/p** makes this a **p**ermanent arrangement for as long as the computer is being used.

7 The **STACKS** line is needed by some programs.

8 There may be other DEVICE lines to set up devices, such as CD ROM drives, communications systems, and driver programs.

When programs add lines to CONFIG.SYS, most of these lines will be of the DEVICE form, adding to the capabilities of the computer.

When a program needs to make use of a device such as a CD-ROM drive, a suitable driver has to be resident in memory, and another DEVICE line will be added to CONFIG.SYS.

You do not necessarily have to understand these lines in the CONFIG.SYS file, but you need to be able to edit the file if required.

When different programs add lines to CONFIG.SYS there is a chance that one will interfere with another. You may then have to alter the relative positions of different lines. Manuals will warn of this if the problem is well-known.

If your computer refuses to start after a new program has been installed, a change to CONFIG.SYS may be the cause. Take a copy of the original version before doing anything that would change the file.

Summary

❑ The **AUTOEXEC.BAT** file is a batch file that runs automatically when the computer is booted.

❑ This file contains the important **PATH** line that enables MS-DOS to find program files in a list of directories.

❑ You can also put in **SET** lines that are used to store parameters that various programs can use.

❑ Other lines are commands that install programs that remain in the memory (TSR programs).

❑ The **MEMMAKER** program alters your AUTOEXEC.BAT file to make the best possible use of memory.

❑ Unlike AUTOEXEC.BAT, the **CONFIG.SYS** file does not use familiar MS-DOS commands.

❑ The CONFIG.SYS file is used early in the booting process to set up the machine to run MS-DOS.

❑ Installing new programs will often cause changes to be made to CONFIG.SYS. These can cause conflicts and you may need to edit CONFIG.SYS so as to shift some lines.

❑ The **DEVICE** line that installs HIMEM.SYS must be placed at or near the top of the CONFIG.SYS file.

14 Self-help

Getting help

You can get quite a lot of useful help from the Help pages of MS-DOS, as Section 6 has shown. If you need detailed information on a command, you can use the HELP command, select the item on which you need information, and print out the pages.

The other form of help, in which you follow a command name with /?, can be very useful if you need a reminder rather than help with understanding what can be done.

It's unusual to get problems that come out of the blue. What you are more likely to find is that problems are associated with installing a new program. These might be apparent immediately - you find that the computer locks up when you try to use it. Others are apparent only later when you try something new, like printing screen contents, for example.

Problems like these are caused by conflicts - a program is trying to use a part of the memory that is occupied by a resident program, for example. This type of thing is unusual nowadays on modern machines and with modern versions of MS-DOS, but we don't all keep up to date.

Problems that can be pinned on the installation of a new program can usually be sorted out, either with reference to the manual, or to the suppliers or manufacturers of the program. A few problems are so well known that you will find them in the README.TXT files of MS-DOS or of the program itself.

Basic steps

1 Look at the abbreviated Help - see if it jogs your memory.

2 Try the extended HELP, print out pages if necessary.

3 Look up the topic in the MS-DOS manual.

4 Look up the subject in independent books of UK origin that deal with MS-DOS.

5 Use the technical help lines of program suppliers for advice on problems connected with specific programs.

6 Look for magazine advice columns which deal with technical problems.

There is always a chance that your computer is odd in some way. Surprisingly, low-cost machines and DIY specials are often the least odd, because they use well-tried and commonly-available parts. It's the manufacturers who think they know better than IBM who often make the odd ones.

The more experience you can get on your side, the better. Reading books helps, and you should take a look at the **Step-by-Step** series from Heinemann-Newtech, and the **Pocket** series from Butterworth-Heinemann.

Magazines are also very useful. Most magazines that cater for newcomers (not all do) run advice and technical help columns, and it often happens that you will see an answer to a query from someone else that helps you considerably.

In particular, look at the excellent **PC Plus** and **PC Answers**, from Future Publishing. These are British magazines and they are geared to helping their readers rather than trying to impress them with displays of advanced knowledge.

Summary

❏ Use the HELP pages of MS-DOS to jog your memory or to provide more detailed information.

❏ Remember that the PC's manual contains the most detailed information on how to set up the machine and on problem solving.

❏ Always print out README.TXT files - they will contain stop-press information that came too late to get into the manuals.

❏ Use the wide range of books and magazines to get more information. Every little helps to build up your understanding of the machine and its programs.

Index